Science
Stage 5
Second Edition

Judith Amery

Boost

HODDER
EDUCATION
AN HACHETTE UK COMPANY

This text has not been through the Cambridge International endorsement process.

Every effort has been made to trace all copyright holders, but if any have been inadvertently overlooked, the Publishers will be pleased to make the necessary arrangements at the first opportunity.

Although every effort has been made to ensure that website addresses are correct at time of going to press, Hodder Education cannot be held responsible for the content of any website mentioned in this book. It is sometimes possible to find a relocated web page by typing the address of the home page for a website in the URL window of your browser.

Hachette UK's policy is to use papers that are natural, renewable and recyclable products and made from wood grown in well-managed forests and other controlled sources. The logging and manufacturing processes are expected to conform to the environmental regulations of the country of origin.

Orders: please contact Hachette UK Distribution, Hely Hutchinson Centre, Milton Road, Didcot, Oxfordshire, OX11 7HH. Telephone: +44 (0)1235 827827. Email: education@hachette.co.uk. Lines are open from 9 a.m. to 5 p.m., Monday to Friday. You can also order through our website: www.hoddereducation.com.

ISBN: 9781398346710

© Judith Amery 2023

First published in 2013

This edition published in 2023 by

Hodder Education

An Hachette UK Company

Carmelite House

50 Victoria Embankment

London EC4Y 0DZ

Impression number   10 9 8 7 6 5 4 3 2 1

Year   2027 2026 2025 2024 2023

Cover illustration by Lisa Hunt, The Bright Agency

Illustrations by Integra Software Services, India

Typeset in India by Integra Software Services Pvt. Ltd, Pondicherry

Printed in the UK

A catalogue record for this title is available from the British Library.

Contents

How to use this book

Cambridge Primary Ready to Go Lessons for Science is a series of print and digital resources providing creative teaching strategies to support the delivery of the new Cambridge Primary Science at Stages 1–6. For each stage, there is a print book (like this one) and a suite of digital resources that you can access online at Boost. (boost-learning.com)

The resources have been structured to reflect Hodder Education's other resources for the Cambridge Primary Science course, with units corresponding directly to those in the Learner's Books, Teacher's Guides and Workbooks; however you can use these independently to support your delivery of the curriculum.

Each unit comprises:

- a set of lesson plans designed to target some of the most challenging aspects of the curriculum
- a set of PowerPoint slides containing starter activities or to support other activities for each lesson (Boost)
- photocopiable worksheets and flashcards to accompany each lesson (Boost)
- knowledge tests for Stages 4–6 (Boost)
- end-of-year tests for Stages 3–6 (Boost).

The lesson plans include the following features to help you structure your teaching.

Prior learning

A short outline of what the learners should be able to do and understand before attempting the unit.

Science in context

Science in context helps learners find out how science is used in everyday life. It helps them to find out how some of the things they use every day work. Jobs which require a scientific background are also introduced to show a range of possible careers. Ideas of how scientific thinking has changed over time help learners understand how scientific developments continue to make our lives better. Consideration is also given to how we can use scientific thinking to protect our world.

Resources

A list of resources, including Boost links for PowerPoints and worksheets for the lesson. Learners get to practise what they have learnt in the lesson.

Starter activity

A whole-class activity (sometimes available on PowerPoint) to prepare learners for the main activity.

Main activities

Activities that promote scientific enquiry and promote thinking and working scientifically.

Digging deeper

Provides opportunities for support or extension.

Wrapping up

Plenary session to draw the lesson to a close and recap the learning objectives.

Assessment for learning

Questions to ask in order to gauge the learners' level of understanding throughout the lesson.

We hope that using these resources will give you confidence and creative ideas in delivering the new Cambridge Primary Science curriculum framework.

Safety

The lessons in this book have been written with safety in mind. However, please ensure that you are aware of and conform to any national, regional or school regulations for safety as you conduct the activities in this book.

Always be aware of skin and food allergies/ intolerances and obtain parental consent for learners to participate in tasting activities. If necessary, carry out a risk assessment of potential hazards before doing the activities. Ensure that learners are aware of safety considerations when carrying out practical activities.

Unit 1 Plant parts

Prior learning

Learners should be able to recall the simple structure of a flowering plant, with reference to roots, stem, leaves and flowers, and know the functions of each plant part. They may also be able to recall the importance of temperature, light and water for healthy plant growth. Learners should know the life processes common to plants: nutrition, growth, movement and reproduction.

Science in context

Lesson 1.1 provides an opportunity for learners to find out about the work of botanists.

1.1 Plant groups

Resources

PowerPoint 1.1; Worksheet 1.1 (Boost); extra copies of Worksheet 1.1 for the extension activity; samples of flowering plants, conifers, ferns and mosses (optional); digital cameras; internet access and/or reference books with information on flowering and non-flowering plants

Starter activity

- Use **PowerPoint 1.1**, slide 1, to show a typical flowering plant.
- With talk partners, ask learners to discuss the characteristics of the first main plant group: flowering plants. (Flowering plants have well-defined root systems, stems, leaves and easily identifiable flowers. They reproduce by producing seeds in their flowers.) This discussion also serves as a good way to discover their prior knowledge at the start of Stage 5.

Main activities

- Use **PowerPoint 1.1**, slides 2–4, to show images of non-flowering plants. These are conifers, ferns and mosses.
- Discuss and observe these in detail as a class and make comparisons.
  - Conifers: often grow into very tall trees with needles instead of leaves. They reproduce by producing seeds inside cones.
  - Ferns: these can also grow into huge tree ferns. Their leaves are called fronds. They reproduce using spores on the back of their fronds.
  - Mosses: these are very small and can be found in damp shade. They produce spores, not flowers, as their means of reproduction. They do not have roots.
- If possible, have samples available of each type of plant to be observed by learners.
- Give out **Worksheet 1.1** and explain to the learners that they need to find an image, take a digital photo or draw a sketch of one example of each type of plant. If real samples are available, the learners could use these as examples. They also need to write brief notes to describe the characteristics of each type of plant. Ask learners to describe the colour, shape, size and any other features of the plants they observe.
- Tell learners whether they should use reference books or the internet for their searches.

Misconceptions

Some learners might think all plants have flowers. Explain that this is not true (as they will discover in this lesson) and that most plants only flower for a short time during their life cycle. Tell learners they will find out a lot more about this in Unit 2.

Some learners might think trees do not flower. Explain that tree blossom is the flowers produced by some trees seasonally.

Support: Before giving out the worksheet, write the names of plants of each type on the worksheet *or* give the learners specific names of plants to research, choosing familiar plants according to your location in the world. Alternatively, allow these learners to work in mixed-ability pairs or groups to carry out this research.

Extension: Challenge these learners to find as many different examples of each plant type as time allows and write them down on extra copies of **Worksheet 1.1**.

Wrapping up

- Explain how these non-flowering and flowering plants are the four main groups that scientists use to classify and identify plants.
- Ask different learners to share their findings and to show their examples.
- If any learners have carried out the extension activity, ask them also to share their findings and examples.
- Explain how some people make a career by becoming a botanist. Use **PowerPoint 1.1**, slide 5, to show a video of what botanists do. Start from 1:10.

Assessment for learning

Ask the learners:
- *What are the four main groups of plants?*
- *Describe and name an example of a conifer, moss, fern or flowering plant.*
- *How is a conifer different from moss?* (Repeat for different pairs of plant types.)

1.2 Classifying flowering and non-flowering plants

Resources

PowerPoint 1.2; Worksheet 1.2 (Boost); extra copies of Worksheet 1.2 for the extension activity; samples of flowering plants, conifers, ferns and mosses (optional); internet access and/or reference books on flowering and non-flowering plants

Starter activity

- Use **PowerPoint 1.1** from the previous lesson (Lesson 1.1) to remind learners about the four main groups of plants: flowering plants, conifers, ferns and mosses.
- Look together at **PowerPoint 1.2**, slide 1, which shows images of plants. The learners will be expected to identify these plants using the key on **Worksheet 1.2** as the Main activity for this lesson.
- Ask the question on the slide: *How do you think some of these plants have been named?* The plants are A, giant fern; B, spoon-leaved moss; C, Scots pine; D, hibiscus; E, corkscrew hazel; F, centipede grass. Often, plants are named based on their external appearance. Ask learners to look closely! For example, corkscrew hazel is twisted, like a corkscrew twist; spoon-leaved moss has leaves shaped like small spoons; centipede grass looks like centipedes.
- Talk about the external observable features of each plant. Tell the learners they will need to use the key on the worksheet to name each plant A–F.

Main activities

- Remind learners that identification keys can be used to find out the names of different plants or animals. Explain how one type of sorting key involves answering a series of questions that will lead you to identify a plant from its external appearance. Each stage either identifies the plant name or directs you to another question. By answering the questions, you can name all the listed plants.

- Give out **Worksheet 1.2** to each learner and show them how to use the key to answer the questions.

- Explain that, by the end, they should have been able to identify each plant on **PowerPoint 1.2**, slide 1, correctly. Explain that trees, such as the corkscrew hazel, are very large flowering plants that produce seeds and then flowers or fruits. Grasses, such as centipede grass, are also flowering plants because they produce grass seeds. Their flowers are not big and bright, however, so they may be less obvious.

Misconceptions

Some learners might not think of trees as flowering plants, due to their size. This lesson helps to address this misconception. Also, some learners might not recognise grasses as flowering plants because they do not produce pretty, coloured flowers. Again, this is addressed in this lesson.

Digging deeper

Support: Work in a small group with these learners, perhaps completing the worksheet as a group. Refer to **PowerPoint 1.2**, slide 1, to help with easier identification.

Extension: Ask these learners to use the internet or reference books to find other plants that would fulfil the criteria of the questions in the key. Ask them to write an answer key and then test their friends! Give them another copy of Worksheet 1.2 to work from.

Wrapping up

- Talk through the answers to the key on the worksheet. Work through each question systematically, asking learners to justify their choice of response each time.

- **Answers:**
  - **A – Giant fern:** this is a fern which reproduces using spores. It has roots, stems and leaves.
  - **B – Spoon-leaved moss:** mosses reproduce using spores. They have no true roots and mainly grow in damp shade.
  - **C – Scots pine tree:** does not produce flowers; its seeds are contained inside cones.
  - **D – Hibiscus flower:** the brightly coloured flowers attract insects to pollinate them.
  - **E – Corkscrew hazel:** this tree produces catkins as flowers which droop down, and this makes it easier for pollen to be carried on the wind. The flowers are not brightly coloured because they do not need to attract insects.
  - **F – Centipede grass:** grasses usually have brown or green flowers or stems and easily sway or bend in the wind. Grasses are also pollinated by the wind and so do not need colourful flowers.

- Explain how keys can help you to identify and name things. Although it is relatively easy to identify a grass, fern or flowering plant, there are actually millions of different types around the world.

Assessment for learning

Ask the learners:
- *What is an identification key used for in science?*
- *What features tell you that a tree is a flowering plant?*
- *How do ferns reproduce?*
- *What do mosses **not** have?*
- *How do you think* [name of plant] *got its name?*

1.3 Parts of a flower

Resources

PowerPoint 1.3; Worksheet 1.3; flashcards (Boost); a collection of real or synthetic flowers, or pictures from the internet or books; hand lenses or magnifying glasses

Starter activity

- If there is time and specimens are available to be picked (always check local laws: in the UK it is illegal to pick wild flowers), organise the learners to go outside and choose a flower for their group or pair to look at. Emphasise that they should only pick flowers where they have been given permission to do so.
- Alternatively, provide a selection of fresh flowers. (Synthetic flowers or photos of different flowers from the internet can be used if fresh specimens are not readily available.)
- Be aware of any plant allergies in the group or learners who might suffer from hay fever.
- Look at some examples of real or synthetic flowers. If there are sufficient samples available, give the learners a flower to examine with their talk partner.
- With talk partners, ask learners to identify the different parts of a flower.
- Share and discuss their responses and find out what vocabulary they might already be familiar with.

Main activities

- Use **PowerPoint 1.3** to show the structure of a flower. Encourage learners to use the correct vocabulary for the parts of a flower.
- Give out **Worksheet 1.3** to use as a reference for the names of different parts of a flower. Ask learners to draw a diagram of the flower they have been observing. Suggest they might like to draw an aerial (looking down) view and a side view to illustrate their observations. Give them a magnifying glass or hand lens to look closely at the flower.

Misconceptions

Some learners might think the function of the petals is merely to make the flower appear attractive, with no idea about the role of petals in plant reproduction. This will be addressed in Unit 2, The life cycle of a flowering plant.

Digging deeper

Support: For these learners, choose a simple flower (perhaps a familiar flower). Write the name of the flower on the worksheet for them in preparation. Ask them to count the numbers of sepals and petals on their flower. Choose a flower that will enable them to count the numbers of petals and sepals easily.

Extension: Give each of these learners, or each pair of learners, a different flower and ask them to compare the numbers of petals, sepals and so on, on each separate flower.

Wrapping up

- Look at the completed diagrams on **Worksheet 1.3**.
- Compare the flowers studied using some similarities and differences observed by the learners; for example: bright, colourful petals, attractive scent.
- Use the flashcards on Boost to test the learners' knowledge of vocabulary for the parts of a flower.

Assessment for learning

Ask the learners:
- *What is the name of the flower you looked at?*
- *What is the function of the petals?*
- *How many sepals did you find?*
- *Do all flowers have the same number of petals?*

1.4 Male and female parts of a flowering plant

Resources

PowerPoint 1.4; Worksheet 1.4 (Boost); tweezers; selection of different flowers suitable for dissection and easy counting of flower parts (this will depend on your location); magnifying glasses or hand lenses; internet access or reference books about flowering plants

Starter activity

- With talk partners, ask learners to talk about the flowers observed in the previous lesson. Ask them to name the different plant parts. Can learners give any functions of petals?
- Use **PowerPoint 1.4**, slide 1, to revise the male parts of a flower and slide 2 to revise the female parts of a flower. Check for correct use of vocabulary: petal, sepal, stamen, anther, filament, carpel, stigma, style, ovary. Explain to learners that they will be looking at the functions of each part in Unit 2, The life cycle of a flowering plant.

Main activities

- Tell learners that, in this lesson, they will be looking at and counting the different parts of a flower. They might have a flower that is the same as or different to those given to other learners.
- Explain to all the learners that they need to pull their flower apart (gently!), using the tweezers provided, and count the different numbers of plant parts in their flower. They should record their observations on **Worksheet 1.4**.

Digging deeper

Support: Work in a small group with these learners or allow them to work in mixed-ability groups to carry out the Main activity.

Extension: Ask these learners to find a flower they like the appearance of on the internet or in a reference book. They should find out about the numbers of sepals, petals, stamens and carpels (stigma, style and ovaries) it has.

Wrapping up

- Talk through the responses for **Worksheet 1.4**. These will be open-ended responses, according to the different flowers that have been observed.
- Ask any learners who have completed the extension activity to share their findings; again, responses will be open ended.
- Explain the following functions of the parts of a flower:
  - the anther – produces and disperses pollen
  - the filament – supports the anther
  - the stigma – the top of the female part of a flower, which receives or collects pollen grains
  - the style – joins the stigma to the ovary
  - the ovary – contains ovules, which eventually turn into seeds.

Assessment for learning

Ask the learners:
- *What are the names of the female parts of a flower?*
- *What are the names of the male parts of a flower?*

1 Unit assessment

- *Name the two main groups of plants.*
- *Give an example of each group of plant.*
- *Name any type of non-flowering plant.*
- *What is a question key used for in science?*

- *Name two groups of plants which reproduce using spores.*
- *Describe conifer leaves and say where a conifer stores its seeds.*

Summative assessment activity

Observe the learners while they complete this activity. You will be able to quickly identify those who appear to be confident and those who might need additional support.

Sorting flowering and non-flowering plants

This activity reveals the learners' understanding of the different characteristics of flowering plants and different types of non-flowering plants: conifers, ferns and mosses.

You will need:
A set of images of flowering and non-flowering plants from the internet or reference books. Alternatively, re-use the PowerPoints from this unit.

What to do

- Give each learner (if there are sufficient resources), pair or small group a set of images to sort. Ask them to group them in as many different ways as possible and to record and explain their groupings each time (for example, flowering/non-flowering; reproduce using seeds/reproduce using spores; grow in damp, shady places/bright places).
- Talk with the learners about their choices. Record their individual responses on a checklist to keep track of their understanding of the main concepts in this unit.

Written assessment
Give learners time to complete **Worksheet 1.5**. The learners should work independently or with their usual in-class support.

Prior learning

Learners should be able to recall that plants need water and light to survive, and the right conditions of temperature, light and water to grow well. They should also know about different habitats and environments, and examples of some plants that can be found in different growing conditions. They might also be able to recall how plants get their energy.

Science in context

Lesson 2.1 enables learners to find out about the effect of the use of pesticides and the impact of this on food production.

2.1 Stages in the life cycle of a flowering plant

Resources

PowerPoint 2.1; Worksheet 2.1 (Boost); sets of labelled cards with the words or phrases describing each stage in the life cycle of a flowering plant: pollination, fertilisation, seed production, seed dispersal, germination. There should be enough sets for the number of groups you choose.

Starter activity

- Arrange the class into pairs or small groups and give each group a set of cards. Ask them to arrange them in order (as a cycle) of what happens in the life cycle of a flowering plant.
- Ask the learners to tell you what happens at the stage written on each card.

Main activities

- Use **PowerPoint 2.1** to introduce the life cycle of a flowering plant. Ask questions such as: *What does this diagram show? Ask learners to describe

what is happening in any stage in the diagram. Does anyone know any special scientific words for what is happening at each stage in the cycle?*
- Discuss as a whole class, compare the learners' answers and address any questions.
- Confirm the order of the stages in the cycle.
  - Germination: seed begins to grow and develops roots and shoots.
  - Growth: shoots get bigger.
  - Flowering: the plant produces one or more flowers.
  - Pollination: pollen is brought to the flower from male anthers and is transferred to the female stigma (usually by insects).
  - Fertilisation: the male pollen grain fertilises the female ovule in the ovary.
  - Seed dispersal: the plant produces seeds, which will grow into new plants. The seeds are scattered to new sites, to take them away from the parent plant.
  - The cycle begins again …
- Give out **Worksheet 2.1** and explain to learners that they should label the correct stages on the diagram. Explain that this differs slightly from the PowerPoint slide image. Challenge them to work out the correct labels together!

Misconceptions

Some learners might think a flower on a flowering plant is not part of the life cycle. Explain that these plants only flower when they are ready to reproduce. This is a specific stage in the life cycle of a flowering plant.

Digging deeper

Support: Work with these learners in completing the rest of **Worksheet 2.1**. Alternatively, allow them to work in pairs or small groups to complete this activity.

Extension: Ask these learners to write a sentence to explain what happens at each stage of the life cycle on the back of **Worksheet 2.1**.

Wrapping up

- Talk through the answers to **Worksheet 2.1** (clockwise from the top): seed production (given), **seed dispersal**, **germination**, **growth**, **pollination**, fertilisation (given).
- Explain that the life process is a cycle, which keeps going round and round. Seeds produce new plants which, in turn, make new seeds and so the plant survives. Compare this to the human life cycle: baby – child – adolescent – adult.
- Make sure the learners know the name of each stage in the life cycle and can remember the correct spelling of each.
- Explain that each stage will be studied in greater depth in the rest of this unit.
- Discuss how the use of pesticides could affect food production (for example, more food could be produced, but chemicals could damage the crops; depending on conditions, there could be more or less food produced).

Assessment for learning

Ask the learners:
- *How can you tell when a seed has germinated?*
- *When a plant grows, what does it produce?*
- *How does pollination usually occur?*
- *What is the process when pollen and ova combine?*
- *What do all green plants need to grow well?*

2.2 Plant parts in pollination

Resources

PowerPoint 2.2; Worksheets 2.2a and 2.2b (Boost); real flowers with lots of pollen on the stamens; sticky tape; hand-washing facilities; internet access or reference books

Starter activity

- Use **PowerPoint 2.2**, which shows a talk about pollination. Watch from 3:19 to the end with the class (although you might like to watch it all on your own first).
- As the class watches the video, stop it at various points and ask the learners, *Which part of the flower does this happen in?* This will prompt discussion about the role of each plant part.
- Explain that, in this lesson, they will be thinking in more detail about what each plant part does in the process of pollination.
- Tell learners that insect pollination is not the only method of pollination; they will find out about other methods in the following lessons in this unit.
- Ask learners: *Have you ever been covered in pollen?* Some of them might have had pollen on their clothes or hands. Invite them to share their experiences if this has ever happened to them. Lilies have lots of deep yellow pollen, which spreads easily. It can also stain quite badly, so some florists remove the stamens so that the pollen cannot stain clothes and soft furnishings.
- Give the learners a real flower and ask them to try to collect pollen from the stamens using sticky tape. Ensure hands are washed carefully afterwards!

Main activities

- Ask the learners to tell you again how insects are attracted to flowers. (Flowers attract insects by being large, colourful and having a pleasant scent/smell.)
- Remind the learners that insect pollination is when insects carry pollen from a plant's anthers (the male part) to their stigmas (the female part), or to the stigmas of other flowers. When an insect visits a flower to feed, the pollen gets shaken off the anthers and some pollen grains may stick to its hairy body or legs. When the insect flies off, the pollen is carried off with it to the next flower it visits. The pollen lands on the stigma of the next flower, which has a sticky surface, and so attaches there. (Bright, perfumed petals also attract birds and bats, as seen the video.)
- Give out **Worksheet 2.2a** to learners who need support. They should cut out the statements and match them with the appropriate image.
- Give out **Worksheet 2.2b** to all other learners and explain that they will use the information on the worksheet to help them complete the facts about the stigma, stamen and ovary.

Misconceptions

Some learners might believe that bees are the only pollinators of flowering plants. Tell them there are many other animal pollinators, including other insects, some small birds, reptiles and mammals.

Digging deeper

Support: Give these learners **Worksheet 2.2a**.

Extension: Ask these learners: *Do different colours of flowers and shapes of petals attract different insects?* Give them internet access or provide reference books with information about insect pollination for them to use for their research. (Responses will be open-ended, depending on the flowers they find.)

Wrapping up

- Invite learners to show their work and discuss it, for both worksheets.
- Ask for contributions from those who might have carried out the extension activity.

Assessment for learning

Ask the learners:
- *What are ova?*
- *What do ova need to be able to grow into seeds?*
- *Where is pollen found?*
- *How does pollen get to the ova?*
- *What happens when the pollen meets the ova?*

2.3 Flowers and fruits

Resources

PowerPoint 2.3; Worksheet 2.3 (Boost); internet access or reference books; examples (real or imitation) of plants with fruits or flowers on them and/or pictures of many different types of fruits, including cucumbers, peppers, tomatoes, nuts in their shells, grains; magnifying glasses or hand lenses; a range of art materials: pencils, paint, paper, collage materials, fabrics and threads

Starter activity

- Ask the learners to work in pairs to identify as many of the fruits and flowers available as they can within a given time limit (pictures and/or samples). Alternatively, present a series of pictures and organise this as a quiz, awarding a small prize for the winning individual, table or team (if this approach is permitted within the rewards system in your school).
- In small groups or as a class, discuss the question, *What is the difference between fruits and flowers?* (Flowers contain the plant's reproductive organs, fruits contain seeds.) Use **PowerPoint 2.3** and talk about the pictures of the fruits and flowers on it: sunflower, jasmine and rice flower, grapefruit, date and rambutan. Ask if learners have seen any of these flowers or eaten any of the fruits.
- Ask the learners to think about the purposes of each and to share their thoughts with the rest of the class.
- This will give you an insight into how much detail regarding flowering plants the learners have remembered from previous work on plants in other stages.

Main activities

- Explain that flowers and fruits are the produce of flowering plants and that it is from these that new plants grow. Flowers contain the plant's reproductive organs; fruits contain seeds.
- Give out **Worksheet 2.3** and ask the learners to draw a storyboard to describe how they think new plants grow from a flower or fruit. Explain that a storyboard is a series of pictures showing the stages of plant growth (seed, small plant, growing plant, plant with fruit or flowers). Start from when the seed is planted.
- Give the learners the opportunity to observe some actual flowers and fruits closely. Use magnifying glasses or hand lenses, if preferred (or available).
- Ask them to make a representation of the flower or fruit they have chosen or been given. Explain that this could be a drawing, painting, collage or textile work, depending on the range of art materials and time available.
- Ask them to make the piece an insect's view (i.e. viewed from close-up) to give a sense of enlarged perspective. The work could be 2D or 3D. It may take more than one lesson to complete.

Biology

Misconceptions

Learners might not understand that the term 'fruit' includes any structure that contains a seed. Show learners pictures of a wide range of fruits (e.g. cucumbers, nuts in their shells, grains, tomatoes, peppers) to explain that, biologically, a fruit is a structure which contains a seed or seeds.

Digging deeper

Support: Support these learners to describe and draw the process in three pictures. Suggest ideas for their artwork or give them fewer alternatives to select from.

Extension: Ask these learners to choose and research the life cycle of a particular flowering plant: one that is native to their country.

Wrapping up

- Ask some of the learners to share their storyboards on **Worksheet 2.3** with the rest of the class. Discuss their pictures to check the learners' understanding.
- Remind the learners that flowers grow from seeds, fruits contain seeds and seeds are the basis of reproduction in flowering plants.

Assessment for learning

Ask the learners:
- *Why do flowering plants have flowers or fruits?*
- *Where do flowers and fruits grow from?*
- *What happens to fruit when it grows?*
- *Why are fruits important for plants?*

2.4 Seeds

Resources

PowerPoint 2.4; Worksheet 2.4 (Boost); selection of fruits with seeds (for example, melon, lemon, orange, kiwi, pomegranate); plastic knives; paper plates or napkins; hand-washing facilities; whiteboard or flipchart and markers; card; paint, paint rollers; scissors; ribbon; glue; gift tags or calendar tabs (if being given as a choice of activity)

Starter activity

- Arrange the learners into pairs and give each pair a piece of fruit. Ensure good hygiene and hand washing before learners handle the fruit. Ask them to find the seed or seeds in the fruit; tell them that they may need to cut the fruit to find the seeds.
- Ask the learners to show the rest of the class their fruit and to describe where the seeds can be found, how many seeds there are (if there are under about 20, they can give specific numbers; where there are a lot of seeds they can estimate whether it is 20–50, over 50 or over 100), their colour and texture, and whether they make a pattern inside or on the fruit. This encourages good observational skills.
- Use **PowerPoint 2.4** to talk about the names of different fruit seeds, such as apple pips, cherry stones, etc. Identify some of the less familiar fruits. Have learners tasted any of these?
- If there are no known allergies or intolerances to the fruit, invite the learners to taste them. Encourage them to try a new fruit if they can. Discuss their personal preferences.

Main activities

- Draw up a tally chart – with assistance from the class – of the learners' favourite fruit from the available fruits. Record the tally chart as shown at the top of **Worksheet 2.4**.
- Demonstrate how to use this information to construct a bar chart. Emphasise the need for a title, labelled axes, appropriate scale and clear presentation.
- Give out **Worksheet 2.4** for the learners to make a tally of the favourite fruits in their small group and also to draw their own bar chart.
- Ask learners who need support to use the data you have already obtained (or give them a selection of data to use).
- Allow the learners to use more cut fruit (where appropriate) to make some prints to decorate a greetings card, a calendar or a gift tag. Place the cut side of the fruit into some paint and press it on a piece of paper. Alternatively, they could design and make their own gift wrap by printing a repeating pattern on a piece of paper.

Misconceptions

Explain that a tomato is a fruit because it has seeds inside it, although most people think of it as a salad vegetable.

Digging deeper

Support: Encourage these learners to work together in a small group and help them to collect their data and use it to draw their bar chart.

Extension: Ask these learners to write three questions about the fruit to accompany their bar chart (for instance, which fruits have the smallest number of seeds, which fruit has more seeds than any other, which fruit has the largest seeds). They will ask other learners to answer these questions. Make sure the learners know the answers to their own questions!

Wrapping up

- Interrogate the learners to elicit information about the bar charts drawn. For example, *What is the favourite fruit in your group? Are there any fruits that only one person liked best? How many more people liked* [name of fruit] *rather than* [name of fruit]?
- Invite the learners to show each other the products they made with the fruit prints.
- Remind them that seeds are necessary for reproduction to produce new flowers or fruits.

Assessment for learning

Ask the learners:
- *Which fruit do we like best as a class?*
- *How many more people prefer* [name of fruit] *to* [name of fruit]?
- *Why do plants have seeds?*
- Invite the learners who completed the extension activity to ask their questions about the bar chart that they have constructed if they have not already done so. If they have obtained answers from other learners already, discuss their responses.

2.5 Seed dispersal

Resources

PowerPoint 2.5; Worksheet 2.5 (Boost); whiteboard or flipchart and markers; large space such as a sports hall or gym; gym mats; source of pre-selected music (a familiar or contemporary piece of music); internet access or reference books

Starter activity

- Take the class into the school hall or gym. Ensure that the learners are wearing appropriate footwear or have bare feet (in line with your school rules). Place the gym mats randomly around the space. When the music plays, the learners can move freely around the hall. When the music stops, they must stand on a mat. Repeat this activity several times until they understand what they have to do.
- When everyone is clear on the rules, start removing a mat each time the music stops. This means that learners will need to crowd on to the remaining mats. Make a rule that if they are not standing with both feet on a mat after the music stops, or if they are the last person to stand on a mat, then they are 'out' and have to miss the rest of the game. The winners are those remaining in the game when only one mat is left.
- In pairs, ask the learners to decide what things green plants need to be able to grow.
- Discuss their answers and clarify that all green plants need air, light, minerals and water.

Main activities

- Discuss the idea of seed dispersal, either in the hall/gym or back in the classroom. Following the Starter activity, introduce the idea that seeds from any plant are in competition with each other to find the best growing conditions. In the game they played, learners were competing for space. Do seeds need to compete for space in the same way?
- Introduce the word 'dispersal', meaning the way that seeds are scattered or spread out away from the parent plant. (The term 'parent

plant' may also be new to some learners.) Use **PowerPoint 2.5**, which shows some different seed dispersal methods.

- Give out **Worksheet 2.5**. Describe to learners how they need to look at the pictures of different seeds and decide how they might be dispersed.

Misconceptions

Some learners might think seeds are only dispersed by the wind. This lesson shows other methods plants might use.

Digging deeper

Support: Help these learners when completing **Worksheet 2.5**.

Extension: Ask these learners to find as many different examples of different methods of seed dispersal as they can, using the internet to search or any reference books available.

Wrapping up

- Talk through the answers to **Worksheet 2.5**.
- **Answers:** Coconuts are scattered on water; jacaranda seed pods explode; castor oil fruits have hooks and so can become attached to animal fur or human clothing; flame of the forest tree seed pods are dispersed by the wind.
- Discuss why not being overcrowded is important for growing seeds, and how if they are too close to the parent plant, the new plants will not survive. The parent plant is bigger and has a well-developed root system, so it will be able to take water from the soil more easily. Larger plants will also overshadow smaller plants, so they might not get enough light to grow well (depending on their preferred growing conditions).

Assessment for learning

Ask the learners:
- *What do all green plants need to grow well?*
- *What is the scientific word for scattering seeds?*
- *What do seeds dispersed by wind usually look like?*
- *Why do growing seeds compete for the things they need?*

2.6 Investigating seed dispersal

Resources

PowerPoint 2.6; Worksheets 2.6a and 2.6b (Boost); internet access or pictures of seeds; hand lenses or magnifying glasses; selection of wind-dispersed seeds (e.g. sycamore; examples will depend on your location); hairdryers or electric fans; measuring tapes or sticks; paper, scissors and paper clips (if making helicopter paper seeds rather than using real seeds); reference books

Starter activity

- Show some examples from the internet or books of different methods of seed dispersal, including wind, water, air and animal. Alternatively, use **PowerPoint 2.5** from the previous lesson as a reminder. Talk about the features of the different types of dispersal.
- Look at some different types of seeds and look at their particular characteristics. Use magnifying glasses to observe the seeds more closely. Ask the learners to decide how the seeds might be carried or spread away from the parent plant (they might talk about hooks, wings, feathery seed parts, size of seed, etc.).

Main activities

- Explain that, in this lesson, the learners will be investigating seed dispersal by wind.
- Working in pairs, ask learners to discuss what characteristics wind-dispersed seeds have. (In general, they are light and often have feathery protrusions or wings.)
- Ask: *Which seed will be dispersed the furthest by wind?* Show the learners the selection of seeds available for use in the investigation.
- Explain that they will be given some different seeds and will need to predict which seed will be dispersed the furthest, giving a scientific reason why. Different groups could be given different seeds or all groups could be given the same seeds to test, depending on what type of seeds you can get and how many are available.

- Working in pairs or small groups, learners will need to decide what they will use as a source of wind. (Choices could include an electric fan, a hairdryer or their own breath.) Learners should consider how to make it a fair test. Prompt them to consider where the seed will be dropped from and how they will measure the distance from the wind source.

- Discuss possible ways of recording their results. They could use a table or chart. *Will you be able to use your results to draw a graph?*

- Give them time to plan and carry out the investigation, working in pairs or small groups. **Worksheets 2.6a** and **2.6b** will help them to plan and write up their investigation.

- Check their plans, giving appropriate guidance where necessary. Learners carry out their investigations once their plans have been checked.

- Alternatively, if different types of seeds are not available, make paper flying helicopter seeds to use instead. The website with full instructions is detailed on **PowerPoint 2.6**.

Digging deeper

Support: Organise these learners to work in mixed-ability groups or provide adult support for the group.

Extension: Challenge these learners to use secondary sources (the internet or reference books) to find as many different examples as possible of plants from around the world whose seeds are dispersed by the wind.

Wrapping up

- Invite different groups of learners to share what they did and to discuss and explain their results and conclusions.

- Discuss the need for dispersal away from the parent plant as a means of survival.

Assessment for learning

Ask the learners:
- *Was your prediction correct?*
- *How did you make the test fair?*
- *Which seed was dispersed the furthest?*
- *Why do seeds need to be dispersed away from the parent plant?*

2.7 Germination

Resources

PowerPoint 2.7; Worksheets 2.7a and 2.7b (Boost); plant pots or small containers for growing seeds in; potting compost; dried beans or peas; water; measuring jugs or cylinders

Starter activity

- Explain to the learners that seeds in themselves are not growing. We say that they are dormant.

- Working in pairs, ask the learners to discuss what the word 'dormant' means. Share your answers as a class.

- Then explain that the first stage in the growth process of a seed is called germination.

- Germination is the stage after seed dispersal in the plant life cycle. Explain that, in this lesson, learners will be thinking about what seeds need in order to germinate and begin to grow.

- Within their pairs, ask the learners to discuss the conditions required for germination to take place.

- Share ideas as a class. (Learners will probably suggest light, water and warmth. Note that only the correct temperature and water are required for germination, but do not tell them this until the end of their investigation; this is what they should find out for themselves.)

Main activities

- Use **PowerPoint 2.7** to show an image of a germinating bean seed.

- Explain that different groups will be given different situations to place some growing seeds in and that the results will be compared to find out the best conditions for germination.

- Decide what conditions you will use. Examples could include in the light or in the dark, with or without water, and in cool or mild temperatures.

- Ask the learners how to make the test fair. The variables to be kept constant will be the type and number of seeds, the size of pot and the amount of compost. If learners agree that the seeds need water to germinate, then the same amount of water should also be poured into each seed-growing pot.

- Discuss and agree the conditions for each group. In pairs or small groups, learners should plant the beans or peas and place the pot in the agreed position and conditions.
- Give out **Worksheets 2.7a** and **2.7b** to help the learners describe their method and record their results and observations.
- Discuss how to record the results in groups and as a class. Learners should observe the pots over a period of at least a week and record observations on a daily basis.

Misconceptions

Most learners will probably think light is essential for germination. This is linked to what they know about what plants need to grow well: water, light and the right temperature. Explain how germination usually takes place deep down in the soil where it is dark.

Digging deeper

Support: Allow these learners to work in mixed-ability groups or in a group with adult support.

Extension: Ask these learners to predict which seeds will germinate first and why.

Wrapping up

- At the end of a week of observing the seeds, discuss what learners have recorded.
- Explain that seeds have enough food already stored in them to germinate. The food stored in the seed is dry. It needs to dissolve before germination occurs, so seeds need water.
- Growth is affected by temperature. Seeds need the correct temperature for them to germinate: some need cold, others warmth.

Assessment for learning

Ask the learners:
- *What kind of seed did you plant?*
- *How did you make the test fair?*
- *Which conditions do you think will be best for germination?*
- *What do seeds need in order to germinate?*

2.8 Evidence of germination

Resources

PowerPoint 2.8; Worksheets 2.8a and 2.8b (Boost); seeds planted in the previous lesson; internet access or pictures from reference books; whiteboard or flipchart and markers

Starter activity

- Use **PowerPoint 2.8**, which has pictures of different seeds from around the world. Some trees and bushes in the Australian desert, such as the pink flannel flower and the midge orchid, need fire to help them germinate! Coconuts only germinate after they have been soaked in salt water for some time. Other seeds only germinate after they have passed through the digestive system of an animal or bird; for example, badgers eat yew berry seeds and African elephants eat figs.
- Give out **Worksheet 2.8a** for the learners to complete and show their understanding of the conditions necessary for successful germination.
- Talk through the answers together as a class, allowing the learners to mark their own work or that of their partner.
- **Answers:**
  1 water
  2 dark
  3 warmth
  4 root
  5 shoot
  6 food
  7 seedling
  8 open-ended response, depending on the seed chosen for the investigation

Main activities

- Working in pairs, ask the learners to think back to the previous lesson and to think again about the *exact* conditions necessary for germination. Discuss and agree with the rest of the class.
- Draw up a class list recording their thoughts. Display this prominently as a reference point for the lesson.

- Allow the learners to observe the seeds they planted previously, record their observations and then share their results and observations with the rest of the class.

- Discuss the fact that, once the seedlings begin to grow, they will need to be in the light. Green plants make their food using energy from light. Allow the learners to choose the most suitable place in the classroom for their seedlings to grow well.

- Give out **Worksheet 2.8b** and explain that they need to use the information and interpret it. This will test some of their scientific skills, as well as their knowledge of what happens when seeds germinate.

Misconceptions

Some learners might think seeds always need soil to germinate. Demonstrate seeds which germinate without soil, for example, by growing cress on cotton wool.

Digging deeper

Support: Provide adult support to help these learners complete the worksheets.

Extension: Ask these learners what would happen if the new seedlings were left in the dark.

Wrapping up

- Talk through the answers to **Worksheet 2.8b**.
- **Answers:**
  1 to make it a fair test
  2 water
  3 peas
  4 roots appeared
  5 to compare and observe signs of germination and growth
- Discuss and rectify any misconceptions. For instance, some learners may still think that light is necessary for germination.

Assessment for learning

Ask the learners:
- *What can you see growing first when a seed germinates?*
- *What can you see develop next?*
- *Where does the seed get its energy for this early growth from?*
- *What do we call a young plant once it has germinated?*

2.9 Conditions for germination

Resources

PowerPoint 2.9; Worksheet 2.9 (Boost); internet access or reference books with diagrams and information about germination; identical plant pots or containers; cotton wool; access to a refrigerator; water; bean seeds; marker pen or sticky labels for labelling the pots

Starter activity

- Ask the learners to think back to the earlier lesson about the life cycle of a flowering plant. Use **PowerPoint 2.9** to revise the life cycle of a flowering plant, recapping on the main events at each stage in the cycle, but not germination.

- Working in pairs, learners should try to answer these questions: *What does germination mean? What conditions do seeds need in order to be able to germinate?*

Main activities

- Explain that, in this lesson, the learners will be interpreting data to show how much they understand about germination.

- With the learners, set up an experiment involving three identical pots with cotton wool in the base of each. Water the cotton wool. Place three bean seeds in each pot and label the pots A, B and C. Water one of the pots again (pot A) and place this in a warm position in the light. Place the second pot (pot B) in the refrigerator. Place the third pot (pot C) in a warm, dark cupboard.

- Discuss the different situations that the seeds are being exposed to for the purposes of this experiment. Explain to the learners that they will be able to observe any changes in the seeds over the next few days.
- Ask the learners to make predictions about what will happen in each situation.
- Observe the pots daily over a school week. Ask learners to record any observations; discuss as a class the best way(s) in which they might do this.
- Give out **Worksheet 2.9** and explain that this contains a set of results from a similar experiment.
- By answering the questions, they will be able to show how much they understand about the process of germination.
- Read through the sheet together and ensure that all learners understand how to complete it.

Misconceptions

Some learners will still think that light is necessary for successful germination. Use the results to explain this.

Digging deeper

Support: Work with this group in completing **Worksheet 2.9**.

Extension: Challenge these learners to compete to grow the healthiest bean plant. Let them decide the criteria for 'healthy' and allow them to plant the beans and demonstrate their ideas.

Wrapping up

- Talk through the learners' responses to **Worksheet 2.9**.
- **Answers:**
  1 The seeds in pot A germinated and started to grow.
  2 Pot B seeds did not germinate, possibly because it was too cold.
  3 Pot C tells us water and the correct temperature are essential requirements for germination, not light.

Assessment for learning

Ask the learners:
- *What conditions did the seeds in pot A have?*
- *What was different for the seeds in pot B?*
- *What was different between pots B and C?*
- *What is essential for germination?*

2 Unit assessment

Questions to ask

- *Why do flowering plants have fruits or flowers?*
- *Why do plants have seeds?*
- *Name four different methods of seed dispersal.*
- *What happens during the process of pollination?*
- *Name the male parts of a flower.*
- *How do you know when germination has taken place?*

Summative assessment activities

Observe the learners while they complete these activities. You will be able to quickly identify those who appear to be confident and those who might need additional support.

Flowering plants

This activity assesses the learners' understanding of the life cycle of a flowering plant.

You will need:
PowerPoint 2.1; a set of labels for each stage in the life cycle, as per Lesson 2.1

What to do

- Working with individual learners, show them the diagram on **PowerPoint 2.1**. Give them the set of labels and ask them to say where each label would go.
- For learners who need extension, ask them to complete the whole cycle and to say what happens at each stage you ask them about.
- For learners who need support, talk about the process on each label if they need help. If this proves too difficult, label all the stages except one. Then ask them about the missing label and what comes before and after it.

Seed dispersal

This activity assesses the learners' applied knowledge of the particular characteristics of seeds dispersed by wind/air, water, animals or explosion.

You will need:
A set of pictures showing seeds that have not been discussed in class

What to do

- For each picture, ask the learners to suggest which method of seed dispersal they think the seed would use and why.
- Record their responses on a class checklist for future reference when writing reports.

Written assessment

Give **Worksheet 2.10a** to all learners who need support. Give **Worksheet 2.10b** to all other learners. The learners should work independently or with their usual in-class support.

Prior learning

Learners should be able to recall the differences between habitats and environments. (A habitat refers to the place in which an organism exists and thrives. The environment is the surroundings the habitat is part of: all the physical, chemical and environmental features that can affect life in a particular habitat.) They might also remember some examples of animals and plants that have adapted to be able to survive and thrive in different environments. They should have some basic knowledge of simple food chains and the roles of predators and prey within them.

Science in context

Lesson 3.1 enables learners to learn about how some animals have adapted over time.

3.1 What is adaptation?

Resources

PowerPoint 3.1; Worksheets 3.1a and 3.1b (Boost); sticky notes; internet access or reference books on animal and plant adaptations

Starter activity

- Display the words 'ADAPT' and 'ADAPTATION'.
- In pairs, learners decide what 'adapt' and 'adaptation' mean.
- Ask them to write their definitions on separate sticky notes and stick them under the relevant displayed term. Gather everyone to read the definitions.
- Lead a class discussion to arrive at an agreed definition. Refer to the glossary in the Learner's Book to check the definitions.
  - Adapt: When a plant or an animal changes to suit its environment.
  - Adaptation: A change made by a plant or animal so it suits where it lives, or the process of making this change.

Main activities

- Explain that this lesson will remind learners about adaptation. Give the learners some examples of ways in which different animals and plants are adapted to their habitat(s).
- Use **PowerPoint 3.1**, slides 1–3, to introduce some animal and plant adaptations. Discuss these as a class and compare the information on the slides. (The detail below is also included on the PowerPoint slide notes).
  - **Slide 1**. **Sloths** move very slowly through trees, which makes them difficult to see. Their fur has algae growing in it, which helps them to camouflage. **Giraffes** have long necks to feed from leaves at the top of trees. Their strong tongues enable them to tear leaves easily from the trees. **Turtles** have flippers (modified hands and feet) to swim and dive effectively.
  - **Slide 2**. The animals shown on this slide are less common or familiar but have some interesting adaptations! Alternatively, this can be used for extension work (see below). **Alaskan wood frogs** need to be able to survive the winter. They have developed the ability to freeze up to 60 % of their bodies. Their heart stops beating and they stop breathing! They can survive temperatures as low as −80 degrees Fahrenheit (−62 °C). **Kangaroo rats** live in deserts. They survive without drinking water. All the moisture they need comes from the seeds they eat. They can jump up to 2.74 m to avoid predators. **Antarctic fish** have antifreeze-like proteins in their blood to prevent them from freezing, helping them to survive in Antarctic temperatures.
  - **Slide 3**. **Cacti** survive desert conditions by having large, fleshy stems that store water. Thorns or spikes instead of leaves help reduce water loss. Spikes also protect cacti from animals who want to eat them to get water from inside them. They have deep roots (taproots) to obtain groundwater. Shallow root systems cover a large surface area to trap any available water. **Rainforest trees** are generally very tall with smooth trunks. They grow tall to compete for light with other plants around them. Their smooth bark allows rain to run down to the roots easily. Some grow special

roots called buttress roots. These have a large surface area and are very useful in supporting such tall trees. Some rainforest trees also have stilt roots that grow down from the tree's branches to the ground and help the tree become more stable.

- Give out **Worksheet 3.1a** to all learners. Explain that they should recall some of the information from the PowerPoint slides to complete the worksheet.

Misconceptions

Some learners might think all plants need the same conditions to grow (usually based on their own experience – the plants growing locally and what conditions they are growing in). Show them a range of plants from different habitats around the world. Secondary sources of information can be used to find out about and show plants that grow and survive in extreme environments.

Some learners might think there are places on Earth where no animals live. Although some environments might appear not to have any animals living in them, animals actually do inhabit most environments. These animals usually have very specific adaptations which enable them to survive in these environments. Examples are Alaskan wood frogs and other animals included on **PowerPoint 3.1**, slide 2. These can be used for reference at the end of the lesson.

Digging deeper

Support: Work with these learners in completing **Worksheet 3.1a**. Allow them to refer back to the PowerPoint slides to help them complete the worksheet.

Extension: Give these learners **Worksheet 3.1b** and ask them to research one of the animals on **PowerPoint 3.1**, slide 2.

Wrapping up

- Talk through the answers to **Worksheet 3.1a**.
- Invite any learners who have completed **Worksheet 3.1b** to share their findings, or use **PowerPoint 3.1**, slide 2, to check their responses.
- Use **PowerPoint 3.1**, slide 4, which shows an emu, an ostrich and a penguin. Explain that, over many generations, ostriches and emus have developed much bigger feet and larger bodies. This means they are no longer able to fly, but they do not need to. Penguins used to have typical bird wings; over time, their wings developed into flippers to help them swim better. This is something that learners could perhaps research for themselves outside the lesson, if they are interested.

Assessment for learning

Ask the learners:
- *What does 'adaptation' mean?*
- *Give an example of an animal and explain how it is adapted to living in its environment.*
- *Give an example of a plant and explain how it is adapted to living in its environment.*

3.2 Common predator adaptations

Resources

PowerPoint 3.2; Worksheet 3.2; flashcards (Boost); extra copies of Worksheet 3.2 for the extension activity; internet access or reference books on animal and plant adaptations

Starter activity

- In pairs, learners should discuss these questions: *What is a predator? What is prey?*
- Ask for their verbal responses and then compare their suggestions with the definitions on the flashcards associated with this lesson.

Main activities

- Explain that, in this lesson, learners will be thinking again about predators and prey, and how they are adapted for these roles.
- Use **PowerPoint 3.2**, slide 1, to show some animals classified as predator or prey: an eagle, a snake, a frog, a bird, a worm and a fox. This can also be used to address possible misconceptions (see below).
- **Eagles** are predators and hunt some animals, including **snakes**.
- Snakes can be prey if hunted by eagles, but are also predators for animals including **frogs**.
- A **blackbird** is the predator for a **worm** and the worm is its prey.
- However, the bird then becomes prey for the predator **fox**!
- Foxes can also be eaten (and thus become prey) by wolves, bears and coyotes, for example.
- This addresses the misconception that animals are only predator or prey; some animals can be both predator **and** prey.
- Use **PowerPoint 3.2**, slide 2, to talk together about all the possible predator adaptations of a tiger. Tigers have nocturnal habits: they hunt at night. Stripy camouflage, very good hearing and sight, and sharp teeth and claws are all predator adaptations. Tigers also have very flexible spines, which help them to pounce on their unsuspecting prey quickly and quietly.

- Give out **Worksheet 3.2** for all learners to complete about predator adaptations.
- Provide reliable internet access and/or reference books for learners to carry out their own research under your guidance, where possible.

Misconceptions

Some learners might think animals can only be predator or prey: encourage them to understand that some animals can be both.

Ask learners to look at animals that are both predator and prey, and think about the adaptations that support them surviving as both predator and prey. (Prey adaptations are covered in the following lesson.)

Digging deeper

Support: Work with these learners in completing **Worksheet 3.2**. Allow them to refer back to the PowerPoint slides to help them complete the worksheet. Alternatively, specify the animal you would like them to focus on, such as a tiger, and ask them to add extra information of their own. If they feel confident, they could suggest a similar animal, such as a lion, or choose an animal from the resources available (reference books or the internet).

Extension: Give these learners an extra copy of **Worksheet 3.2** and ask them to complete it for a second predator animal they would like to find out about.

Wrapping up

- Invite some of the learners who needed support to share their answers to **Worksheet 3.2**. Discuss with the learners whether there are any other features they could add.
- Invite any learners who have completed extra worksheets to share their responses also.

Assessment for learning

Ask the learners:
- *What is a predator?*
- *What is prey?*
- *What are the predator adaptations in a [name of animal]?*

3.3 Common prey adaptations

Resources

PowerPoint 3.3; Worksheets 3.3a and 3.3b (Boost); internet access and/or reference books on animal and plant adaptations

Starter activity

- Ask learners: *What is prey?* This will recall prior knowledge from the previous lesson. Refer to the vocabulary cards for revision purposes, if necessary.
- Ask learners to give some examples of animals that are prey for other animals. Refer back to the previous lesson for some examples.

Main activities

- Explain that, in this lesson, learners will be thinking again about prey and how their features have been adapted to prevent them being caught by predators.
- Use **PowerPoint 3.3** to identify different characteristics that help prey animals escape from or hide effectively from possible predators. Ask learners to name examples of animals that fit each different characteristic.
- **Body built for speed**: These creatures are streamlined to enable them to run fast to escape their predators. Examples include antelope and deer.
- **Camouflage**: The chameleon is perhaps the best example of this. It can change the colour and pattern on its skin to provide camouflage against its background. This helps it to escape predators and to hide from its prey.
- **Eyes on the side of their head**: This gives animals a wider field of vision, so they can see all around them and are able to notice predators creeping up or approaching them. Examples include chickens (predated on by foxes or badgers), cows (predated on by wolves and grizzly bears in North America), horses (predators include cougars, wolves or bears) and zebra (predators include lions, leopards and Nile crocodiles).
- **Herd animals**: In a group they can make others in the herd aware of danger, and stronger members can help protect younger and weaker members. Examples of herd animals are wildebeest and buffaloes.
- Give out **Worksheet 3.3a** about prey adaptations for all learners to complete.
- Provide reliable internet access and/or reference books for learners to carry out their research.

Misconceptions

Remind learners of the previous lesson, where they discovered that some animals can be both predator and prey. Refer back to **PowerPoint 3.2** if needed.

Digging deeper

Support: Work with these learners in completing **Worksheet 3.3a**. Allow them to refer back to the PowerPoint slide to help them complete the worksheet. The learners could be organised to work in a mixed-ability pair or group to research animals to complete **Worksheet 3.3a**.

Extension: Give these learners **Worksheet 3.3b** to record their findings about other prey adaptations of interest to them.

Wrapping up

- Talk through learners' responses to **Worksheet 3.3a**.
- Address any misconceptions.
- Invite any learners who have completed **Worksheet 3.3b** to share their responses.

Assessment for learning

Ask the learners:
- *Name an animal that has the prey adaptation of having its eyes on the side of its head.*
- *How does camouflage help prey animals to survive?*
- *What are the prey adaptations in a [name of animal]?*
- *What do we call animals who live in groups? Why is this useful to prevent them being preyed upon?*

3.4 Imaginary animals

Resources

PowerPoint 3.4; Worksheets 3.4a and 3.4b (Boost); dice numbered 0, 1, 2, 4, 6 and 8

Starter activity

- Remind learners that different animals live in different habitats. This is because they have adapted to the conditions in that habitat.

Main activities

- Explain that animals have adapted in a number of ways:
  - how they move; for example, wings for flying (dragonflies), many legs for running fast (millipedes)
  - features for escaping predators; for example, bright colours (butterflies), hard shells (snails), stings (wasps), camouflage (stick insects)
  - how they hunt other animals; for example, making traps (spiders' webs), using stings (scorpions)
  - how they attract a mate; for example, fighting (male rhinoceros beetles) or displaying magnificent tails (peacocks).
- Explain that, in this lesson, learners will design new animals. They will roll a dice to help them decide on the main features of their animals.
- Use **PowerPoint 3.4**, which shows a version of **Worksheet 3.4a**. Explain to the learners what they will be doing.
- Show the learners how to draw the animal, labelling its key features, the number of legs, wings, etc.
- Roll the dice four times.
- For each roll, decide where to put this number; for example, if the first roll is a four, you could choose to give your animal four wings.
- Once your animal is complete, ask the learners to help you think of additional information about it, for example:
  - Where does it live?
  - How has it adapted to this habitat?
  - What colour is it?

- What skin covering does it have (for example, feathers, scales, fur)?
- How large is it?
- What does it eat?
- How does it protect itself?
- Give each learner **Worksheet 3.4a** and ask them to create their own imaginary animal in the same way. Then ask them to draw and label their imaginary animal.
- Ask them to talk about their animal in pairs. Learners should ask each other questions such as:
  - *How does it move?*
  - *How does it capture its food?*
  - *How does it protect itself?*
  - *How does it attract a mate?*

Misconceptions

Remind learners that there are animals that can live and survive in almost every environment on Earth because of their specific adaptations.

Digging deeper

Support: Give these learners **Worksheet 3.4b**. This worksheet contains further questions to help them describe their animal in more detail.

Extension: Encourage these learners to think about the habitat their animal lives in and how it is adapted to this habitat.

Wrapping up

- Ask some learners to show and share their pictures of the animal they have created.
- Ask the other learners if they think this creature would survive in the real world. Ask: *In what ways has this animal adapted to its habitat?*

Assessment for learning

Ask the learners:
- *How would you describe your imaginary animal?*
- *What type of habitat does your animal prefer?*
- *How is it suited to this habitat?*

3 Unit assessment

Questions to ask

- *What is a predator?*
- *What is prey?*
- *How can an animal be both predator and prey?*
- *Can you name some animals that live in the local environment?*

- *Can you talk about the habitat in which they live?*
- *Can you explain how an animal is suited to its environment?*

Summative assessment activities

Observe the learners while they complete these activities. You will be able to quickly identify those who appear to be confident and those who might need additional support.

Create a super bug

This activity encourages the learners to think about how well animals are adapted to their habitat.

You will need:
Modelling clay of different colours

What to do
- Ask learners to create their own super bug using modelling clay.
- While they are making their bugs, question them about the decisions they are making:
  - *Why did you choose that body?*
  - *What are its good points?*
  - *Does it have any weaknesses?*
  - *How does your bug move?*
  - *What does it eat?*
  - *How does your bug protect itself?*
- Ask the learners to draw the bug and add labels to explain how it is adapted.

Super bug trump cards

This game enables the learners to talk about how animals are adapted to their habitat.

You will need:
Blank cards (A4 card cut into four pieces); pencils; colouring pencils or felt-tip pens

What to do
- Provide each learner with four blank cards and ask them to create four super bugs.
- They should draw and colour them carefully, and label their special features.
- Ask the learners in pairs to discuss each bug and to agree on their statistics for strength, speed, attack, defence and agility. They should write these numbers on each card.
- This will create a pack of cards that the learners can use to play trumps (see below).

Playing super bug trumps

This game enables the learners to talk about how animals are adapted to their habitat.

You will need:
Super bug trump cards from previous activity

What to do
- The learners should play in pairs. They should combine their sets of cards and shuffle them. One learner deals out the cards face down. Each learner should look at their top card but not show it to their opponent.
- One of the learners should choose one of the statistics that they think is good for their bug and read this out; for example, 'defence: 19'. Whoever has the super bug with the highest number for defence wins both cards.
- Play continues until one learner runs out of cards.

Written assessment

Distribute **Worksheet 3.5**. The learners should work independently or with their usual in-class support.

Unit 4

Digestion in humans and other animals

4.1 The human digestive system

Resources

PowerPoint 4.1; Worksheets 4.1a and 4.1b (Boost)

Starter activity

- Use **PowerPoint 4.1**, slide 1, to show a diagram of the human digestive system. Ask learners to name any parts they can remember. Refer to all the words on the vocabulary list for this lesson: anus, mouth, oesophagus, large intestine, small intestine and stomach.

- In pairs, ask them to discuss the job (function) of each of these parts. (This will be dealt with in greater detail in other lessons in this unit.)

- If necessary, refer them to the glossary in the Learner's Book to find meanings for all these words and phrases.

Main activities

- Explain to learners that, in this lesson, they will be finding out more about the process of digestion in the human body.

- Show the video on **PowerPoint 4.1**, slide 2, to describe the digestion process. (Note that some of the words that appear on the screen use US spellings (such as esophagus) and some of the terms are in Spanish.)

- Discuss each stage in the process. Stop the video at appropriate times throughout to talk about the different stages in the process.

- Notes from **PowerPoint 4.1**, slide 2: Digestion starts when food is chewed in the **mouth** before being swallowed. The **oesophagus** is a tube which carries the food from the mouth to the **stomach**. In the stomach, food is broken down by stomach acid. In the **small intestine**, food is broken down further into small molecules and these are absorbed into the body. The **large intestine** is where undigested food collects and makes faeces.

- Give out **Worksheet 4.1a** to learners who need support and **Worksheet 4.1b** to all other learners. Explain that they need to be able to use the vocabulary to identify the different parts in the digestive system. For learners who need support, this vocabulary is listed on **Worksheet 4.1a**. Learners completing **Worksheet 4.1b** will be expected to recall and use the relevant vocabulary. Remind these learners that they can refer to the glossary in the Learner's Book for spellings and/or to check definitions.

Misconceptions

Some learners might think food is absorbed in the stomach. This is not quite true – the stomach churns food and adds stomach acid. This will be explained in more detail in the next lesson (4.2 The digestive system).

Digging deeper

Support: Give these learners **Worksheet 4.1a**, which includes all the vocabulary required to complete the task. Guide and help them to read these words if necessary.

Extension: Give these learners **Worksheet 4.1b** to complete. In preparation for the next lesson, ask them also to think about the possible functions of each component.

Assessment for learning

Ask the learners:
- *Where does the process of digestion start?*
- *What is the name of the tube that carries food from the mouth to the stomach?*
- *Where does food go to once you have swallowed it?*
- *What is the main process that happens in the small and large intestines?*

Wrapping up

- Talk through the answers to **Worksheets 4.1a** and **4.1b** by asking different learners to name the various parts of the digestive system.

4.2 The digestive system

Resources

PowerPoint 4.2; Worksheet 4.2 (Boost); small pieces of fruit; a plastic bag containing glue and small fruit pieces (tightly sealed); 5 m of wide plastic tubing; 7 m of narrow plastic tubing

Starter activity

- Give the learners a small piece of fruit to taste and eat. (Check for any food allergies before giving the learners food to eat in class.) Ask them to think about the journey that this piece of food will take through their body.

- Ask them to think about what is happening in their mouth as they eat: the teeth cut and bite the food, they chew to make it more liquid, saliva softens it and makes it easier to swallow. They taste it! Discuss these things as the learners eat.

Main activities

- Explain that the digestive system is responsible for digesting our food by breaking it down into the nutrients we need to stay alive.

- Ask the learners to discuss with talk partners where our food goes after we swallow it (down the throat to the stomach) and what happens to it there (it gets churned up and stomach acid is added to it to break the food down further). Refer to **PowerPoint 4.2** to rewatch the YouTube clip on digestion if you think it is necessary here.

- Demonstrate the churning action of the stomach by using some thick liquid (such as glue) in a tightly sealed plastic bag with a few solid pieces

of fruit in it. Move it around, similar to clothes in a washing machine.

- Show the plastic tubing lengths so that the learners can actually see how long the intestines are. Talk about how the intestines are coiled up and tucked neatly inside the abdomen. Challenge the learners who need extension to try to coil both pieces of tubing so that they would fit inside an adult body!

- Give out **Worksheet 4.2** to all learners.

Digging deeper

Support: Work with these learners to complete **Worksheet 4.2**.

Extension: Give these learners the task of arranging the plastic tubing into a suitable coiled shape to fit inside an adult.

Wrapping up

- Ask some of the learners to show their labelled diagrams of the digestive system and explain what happens at each stage.

Assessment for learning

Ask the learners:
- *Where does digestion start?*
- *Which are the major organs in the digestive system?*
- *What happens in the mouth?*
- *How does the stomach start to digest the food we eat?*
- *What happens as food travels through the intestines?*

4.3 The process of digestion

Resources

PowerPoint 4.1, slide 2 (from Lesson 4.1); PowerPoint 4.3; Worksheets 4.3a and 4.3b; sets of flashcards (enough for one set per pair or small group) (Boost)

Starter activity

- In pairs or small groups, ask learners to sort the flashcards into the order of the process of digestion. This should serve as a good reminder of the previous session.
- Show **PowerPoint 4.1**, slide 2, so that the learners can check their responses.

Main activities

- Explain to learners how, in this lesson, they will be finding out more detail about each stage involved in the process of digestion in the human body.
- Ask learners what the function of each part of the digestive system is. Use **PowerPoint 4.3**, slides 1–6, to elaborate on what happens at the different stages of digestion.
  - **Slide 1, Mouth:** produces saliva to moisten food and begin the process of digestion. Mechanical action is provided by the teeth grinding, cutting and chewing food. Chemical digestion is activated by the saliva.
  - **Slide 2, Oesophagus:** a muscular tube which passes food from the mouth when it is swallowed, down to the stomach.
  - **Slide 3, Stomach:** a muscular bag which churns the semi-liquid food with stomach acid and breaks the food down even more so it is digested before absorption.
  - **Slide 4, Small intestine:** the process of digestion is completed here and then digested food is absorbed into the bloodstream for nutrients to be carried around the body.
  - **Slide 5, Large intestine:** water is absorbed into the body. Undigested food, such as high-fibre food, is collected and forms faeces (solid human waste).
  - **Slide 6, Anus:** the exit point from the human body for faeces. Solid waste is passed out of the body through the anus when you go to the toilet.
- Give out **Worksheet 4.3a** to all learners who need support. This has the stages of digestion in the correct order.
- Give out **Worksheet 4.3b** to all other learners.

Misconceptions

Some learners might think food is absorbed in the stomach. Absorption actually takes place in the small and large intestines.

Digging deeper

Support: Give these learners **Worksheet 4.3a**. This contains the correct order for the process of digestion. Help these learners with reading and writing, especially the correct spelling of the main vocabulary words. Help them to use the word cards when writing their responses.

Extension: Give these learners **Worksheet 4.3b**. This has a more open-ended approach and requires them to remember the order of the stages in the process of digestion.

Wrapping up

- Talk through the answers to **Worksheets 4.3a** and **4.3b**. Refer back to the earlier notes or the notes on the PowerPoint slides. Model correct use of the relevant vocabulary.
- Make sure the learners understand that digestion takes place in the mouth, stomach and small intestine. Then remind them that absorption takes place in the small and large intestines.

Assessment for learning

Ask the learners:
- *What does saliva do?*
- *What happens in the stomach?*
- *What scientific process takes place in the large and small intestines?*
- *Where does solid waste leave the body?*

ml。

Biology

4.4 Digestion in other animals

Resources

PowerPoint 4.4; Worksheet 4.4 (Boost); live earthworms, if available; magnifying glasses; Petri dishes; reference books or internet access

Starter activity

- In pairs or small groups, ask learners to think about what vertebrates are. This serves as good revision. (Vertebrates are living things with a spine, so humans are vertebrates.)
- Use **PowerPoint 4.4**, slide 1, to compare the learners' responses with this definition. Can learners recall another name for the spine? (backbone).

Main activities

- In this lesson, learners will be learning about the digestive systems in different animals.
- Talk about the digestive system in an invertebrate – an animal without a spine or backbone – such as a worm. Use **PowerPoint 4.4**, slide 2, to show the digestion process. Explain how the earthworm eats stones. These get ground up in the gizzard. The food then moves into its intestines and digestive fluids are released. Digested food is then absorbed and carried around the rest of its body.
- Talk about the details that are similar in the digestive system of an earthworm and a human (the process is similar, except that the earthworm has a gizzard, not an oesophagus).
- Organise learners into pairs or small groups and then give out the magnifying glasses and live earthworms for learners to observe. Make sure learners do not touch the earthworms and, for safety reasons, make sure they wash and dry their hands carefully before and after this activity. Alternatively, use the video on **PowerPoint 4.4**, slide 3. This video shows some live earthworms and shares some interesting facts about them.
- Show the video on **PowerPoint 4.4**, slide 4, entitled 'How do animals digest food?' This video shows how barn owls and cows digest their food differently to humans.

- Give out **Worksheet 4.4** to all learners. Explain that they need to complete the sentences and draw a labelled diagram of an earthworm. They may need to look at a book or the internet to be able to add labels to their diagram.

Misconceptions

Some learners might think earthworms have eyes. The video about worms explains how worms use their whole body to detect light.

Digging deeper

Support: Organise these learners into mixed-ability groups to complete **Worksheet 4.4** or work with them to discuss their answers before they complete the worksheet.

Extension: Give these learners an opportunity to carry out internet research – in class or for homework if there is not enough time – to make an interesting facts list about earthworms. Facts could include what they eat and when they are most active. You could direct learners to the video on **PowerPoint 4.4**, slide 3, if this has not been used in the lesson.

Wrapping up

- Talk through the learners' responses on **Worksheet 4.4**, making sure learners understand that the digestive system in any animal has three main functions:
  - to break down food
  - to absorb nutrients from food
  - to get rid of waste.
- Check they understand that many vertebrates have very similar digestive systems.

Assessment for learning

Ask the learners:
- *What is the purpose of a gizzard for an earthworm?*
- *How is the digestive system of an earthworm similar to that of a human?*
- *Give one way in which the digestive system of an owl is different from that of a human.*
- *What is different about the digestive system of a cow?*

4.5 A balanced diet

Resources

PowerPoint 4.5; Worksheets 4.5a, 4.5b and 4.5c (Boost); internet access

Starter activity

- Display **PowerPoint 4.5**, slide 1, and ask learners to identify any foods on the slide that they like or dislike.
- Perhaps discuss what makes their choices tasty or not.
- Ask: *Do we tend to eat more of the foods we like than dislike?*

Main activities

- Show **PowerPoint 4.5**, slide 2, and ask learners to discuss with their talk partner why the plate has been divided in this way.
- Explain that, in this lesson, they will be thinking about the need for a balanced diet in contributing to a healthy lifestyle.
- Explain how this balanced plate can help us to choose a healthy diet. The large segments contain food that we need to eat regularly and the smaller segments show food items that we do not need so much of. The smallest segment shows foods that can be damaging to our health – those high in fat or sugar – and that we should only eat occasionally.
- Explain how each of the food groups helps our bodies:
  - Bread, other cereals and potatoes give us energy.
  - Fruit and vegetables keep us healthy and help our digestive system.
  - Meat, fish and alternatives help our bodies to grow and repair themselves.
  - Dairy products keep our bones and teeth strong and healthy.
  - Foods high in sugar and fat give us a lot of energy (calories) but are not very healthy for us.

- Highlight that a balanced diet is obtained over a period of time, not necessarily at every meal.
- Give all learners **Worksheet 4.5a** and ask them to write in the different sections examples of foods which could be in that food group.
- Ask the learners to carry out internet research into jobs in the food industry; for example, food critic, food blogger, chef, nutritionist, flavour chemist, food photographer. They can then choose one of particular interest to them.

Misconceptions

People who follow special diets, perhaps for health or religious reasons, need to make good food choices. Explain how, as humans, we have teeth that enable us to eat fruit, vegetables and meat if we choose to. Make clear that diet choices can be a personal or family choice and that parents generally make food choices for their families. As we grow older, we become able to make food choices for ourselves and some people may choose to change their diet.

Digging deeper

Support: Give these learners **Worksheet 4.5b** to complete, with **Worksheet 4.5a** for reference to help them complete it.

Extension: Give these learners **Worksheet 4.5c**.

Wrapping up

- Discuss with the learners any food items they were not sure where to place.
- Show the balanced plate on **Worksheet 4.5a** and ask them to compare it to their diet.
- Discuss how each food group benefits our bodies.

Assessment for learning

Ask the learners:
- *Explain how the different food groups help our bodies.*
- *Explain how to have a balanced diet.*

4 Unit assessment

- *What is a vertebrate?*
- *What scientific process allows humans and animals to obtain nutrients from their food?*
- *Describe the journey of food through your digestive system.*

- *What is similar between human and animal digestive systems?*
- *Name something different in another animal's digestive system, for example, an owl or a cow.*
- *Why is a balanced diet important for keeping us healthy?*

Summative assessment activities

Observe the learners while they complete these activities. You will be able to quickly identify those who appear to be confident and those who might need additional support.

The process of digestion

This activity provides an opportunity for learners to demonstrate their knowledge of the order of the process of digestion.

You will need:

The vocabulary word cards prepared for Lesson 4.3

What to do

- Ask learners individually to sort the word cards into the order of the process of digestion. Record their responses to check their understanding.
- If they are unsure about the order, question them to check until they are sure.

Digestion in other animals

This activity provides an opportunity for learners to share their knowledge about the digestive system of another animal and compare it with their own.

You will need:

Images of an earthworm, a barn owl or a cow; paper and pencils

What to do

- Ask individual learners to choose one of the images available.
- Then ask them to draw a mind map of everything they can remember about the digestive system of the animal they have chosen.
- When they have finished, ask them the following questions:
  - *What is the main job of the digestive system in any animal?* (to break down food)
  - *What does the digestive system get for your body from the food?* (nutrients)
  - *What happens at the end of the digestive process?* (the body gets rid of waste)
  - *What is the same about the digestive system of the animal you have chosen and your own digestive system?* (answers will vary depending on the animal chosen)
  - *What is different about the digestive system of the animal you have chosen compared to your digestive system?* (answers will vary depending on the animal chosen)

Written assessment

Distribute **Worksheet 4.6**. The learners should work independently or with their usual in-class support.

Unit 5 States of matter

Learners should be able to recall the three states of matter as solids, liquids and gases. They should also be able to recall particle models for both solids and liquids. They might recall the three states of water: ice, water and water vapour. It would be helpful to check their prior knowledge on this as a basis for planning new learning.

Science in context

Lesson 5.2 provides an opportunity for learners to research some everyday uses of some of the most common gases.

5.1 Solids, liquids and gases

Resources

PowerPoint 5.1; Worksheet 5.1 (Boost); internet access or reference books about changes of state in everyday materials

Starter activity

- This activity is designed as revision of prior knowledge about particle models in both solids and liquids.
- Use **PowerPoint 5.1**, slide 1, to show the particle model for a typical solid. Talk about the arrangement of the particles, how they vibrate and how they behave. Learners should understand that the particles in a solid do not move around freely and that solids have a fixed shape. Ask learners to name some common everyday solid materials in the room. Examples could include glass, plastic and wood.
- Use **PowerPoint 5.1**, slide 2, to show the particle model for a typical liquid. Compare the arrangement of the particles here with the particle model for a solid shown on the previous

PowerPoint slide. (The particles in a liquid are not in fixed positions and can move around each other more freely. This quality enables liquids to be poured.)

Main activities

- Explain how, in this lesson and unit, learners will find out about gases and the particle model of gases. (Learners may have covered this in earlier work on states of matter; however, it is at Stage 5 where the focus is on gases in particular.)
- In pairs, learners discuss what a particle model for a gas would look like. Show **PowerPoint 5.1**, slide 3.
- Give out **Worksheet 5.1** to all learners to complete particle model diagrams for solids, liquids and gases.

Misconceptions

Some learners using the particle model may draw small gaps between the particles in a liquid. In fact, the particles in a liquid are in contact with at least one other particle, although they are not arranged in a regular pattern or order. There are only gaps between particles in the particle model for a gas. It is important to address this common misconception at this stage.

Digging deeper

Support: Allow these learners to work with a friend or work with them in a small group to complete **Worksheet 5.1**.

Extension: Ask these learners to research, using the internet or books, what happens in the particle model as a substance changes state, for example, from solid to liquid to gas.

Wrapping up

- Talk through the answers to **Worksheet 5.1** with reference to the PowerPoint slides used earlier in the lesson.

- Ask some learners who researched the particle models: *What causes changes of state?* This explanation does not need to be detailed. For instance, you could say that energy from heat separates the particles to make a solid melt and turn into a liquid. On further heating, the liquid gains more energy and the particles move as far apart as possible. The substance becomes a gas.

Assessment for learning

Ask the learners:
- *How are the particles arranged in a solid?*
- *What is different about the arrangement of particles in a liquid compared to a solid?*
- *Describe the particle model for a gas. How are the particles arranged?*

5.2 Gases all around

Resources

PowerPoint 5.2; Worksheets 5.2a and 5.2b (Boost); two glass or plastic bottles with tops on (one empty and one filled with water); transparent bowl or sink full of water; internet access or reference books about everyday uses of common gases

Starter activity

- Show the learners the two sealed bottles: one empty and one filled with water. Ask them: *What is inside each bottle?* (One contains water and the other bottle contains air.)
- Place the empty bottle underwater and remove the top, asking the learners to watch carefully.
- In pairs, ask them to discuss what they observe. (If the bottle is open-end down, the water does not go into the bottle unless you tilt it. When this happens, air bubbles come out and water goes in.)
- Bring the bottle out of the water and ask the learners what is inside the bottle now. (water)
- Tip the water out and put the top back on, then ask again what is inside. (air)
- Make sure learners understand that the bottle has air inside it and that air is a gas. When the top was removed underwater, the gas escaped as air bubbles.

Main activities

- Explain how some substances exist at room temperature as gases and that, in this lesson, the learners will be learning the names of some of the most common gases. Explain how they will be learning about the uses of the main gases which make up air. These are nitrogen, oxygen and carbon dioxide.
- Use **PowerPoint 5.2**, slide 1, which shows the different everyday uses of some common gases, including an oxygen cylinder like those used in hospitals. Talk about why oxygen is important – we need it to breathe! Carbon dioxide produces the bubbles in fizzy (carbonated/sparkling) drinks; hydrogen is used in rocket fuel because it ignites (catches fire) so easily; nitrogen is used extensively in food packaging to make some foods last longer, such as bagged salads.
- Give learners who need support **Worksheet 5.2a** to complete with everyday uses of common gases. Give all other learners **Worksheet 5.2b**, which is more open-ended and allows them to include details they already know or can research to find out.

Misconceptions

Some learners are not easily convinced that gases exist, because many gases are invisible most of the time! Use the example of bubbles in a fizzy drink containing carbon dioxide. Explain how the bubbles contain gas and float because they are light.

Digging deeper

Support: Allow these learners to refer to the **PowerPoint 5.2** slide to help them remember some everyday uses of some of the most common gases.

Extension: Ask these learners to research other examples of how some everyday gases might be used. Provide reliable internet access or relevant reference books to do this. Alternatively, give this as a homework activity.

Wrapping up

- Talk through possible answers to everyday uses of common gases. These could include oxygen for breathing and in scuba diving; carbon dioxide in baking (yeast, baking powder and baking soda all produce carbon dioxide during the cooking or baking process); nitrogen used in the manufacture of stainless steel, in pharmaceuticals and in electronics manufacturing; hydrogen used to create ammonia in fertilisers, in the welding process and in extracting metals from metal ores (there are other examples beyond these).

Assessment for learning

Ask the learners:
- *Name a common gas which has several everyday uses.*
- *How is carbon dioxide commonly used?*
- *Why is oxygen important for humans?*
- *Give one use of either nitrogen or hydrogen.*

5.3 Melting and boiling points of water

Resources

PowerPoint 5.3; Worksheets 5.3a and 5.3b (Boost); thermometers; kettle or heat source for boiling water; ice cubes; temperature sensor (if available); graph paper

Starter activity

- In pairs, ask learners to discuss whether they can recall the boiling point or melting point of water.
- Use **PowerPoint 5.3**, slide 1, to ask learners to make predictions about the graph showing the measurement of the boiling point of water. Then tell them that the temperature goes up 10 °C every 30 seconds.
- Use **PowerPoint 5.3**, slide 2, for learners to predict possible temperature rises to complete the table. Accept any answers between 71 to 80 and 81 to 90 °C to complete the table.

- Take this opportunity to explain how making predictions is an important part of thinking and working scientifically.

Main activities

- These activities can be carried out in a single lesson or you might choose to do them over more than one lesson.
- Give out **Worksheets 5.3a** and **5.3b** to all learners. Alternatively, just give out the worksheet for the activity to be carried out in this lesson.
- Explain how the learners should record the temperatures of both melting ice and boiling water. Talk through the instructions for doing this as shown on each worksheet.
- Demonstrate taking the temperature of boiling water yourself (or ask an adult helper do it), for safety reasons.
- Ask some of the learners to measure the temperatures as the water boils, under close adult supervision, and record this on **Worksheet 5.3b**.
- Demonstrate how to use a temperature sensor if one is available. Make a mixture of ice and water. Use the temperature sensor to record the temperature of the mixture at ten-minute intervals over one to two hours.

Misconceptions

Some learners might think ice, water, steam and water vapour are different substances. Throughout this unit, take time to explain each different change of state as it is demonstrated or observed.

Digging deeper

Support: Work in a small group with these learners or allow them to work in mixed-ability groups.

Extension: Ask these learners to plot a graph using the results presented for discussion in the Starter activity. Ask them to use it to explain what happened to the water when it boiled.

Wrapping up

- Discuss the learners' results and take an average for the melting and boiling temperatures of water.
- Analyse the results produced by the temperature sensor (if used).
- Ask: *What do these results tell you about the melting temperature of ice and room temperature?*
- Predict what the results might be if the room were 10°C hotter or colder.
- Explain that the boiling point of pure water (at standard temperature and pressure, but they do not need to know this) is 100°C. They need to remember this fact.
- The melting point of ice (frozen water), when it turns to liquid from ice, is 0°C (again, in standard conditions). The learners also need to remember this fact.
- Discuss what the bar chart on **Worksheet 5.3b** shows: when the water reaches its boiling point, the graph plateaus (flattens out).

Assessment for learning

Ask the learners:
- *What is the meaning of temperature?*
- *Why is it useful to take an average of results?*
- *What temperature does ice melt at?*
- *What is the boiling point of water?*

5.4 What is evaporation?

Resources

PowerPoint 5.4; Worksheet 5.4 (Boost); bottle of perfume or air freshener (or something strongly scented; make sure to check whether there are any allergies among the learners, especially if using air fresheners); heat source (for example a candle, a nightlight or a spirit burner); container of water, such as a cup of boiling water with steam coming off it; measuring cylinder; large space

Starter activity

- Put the learners in pairs and then ask them to close their eyes. Leave a bottle of perfume, fragrance or something that is strongly scented open near to them for a few minutes.
- Ask them to raise their hand when they think they know why you have asked them to close their eyes.
- Ask the pairs to discuss why they are able to detect the fragrance. (It evaporates or is able to travel through the air.)
- Talk about other things that they like the smell of or even unpleasant smells that they can sometimes detect!
- Ask the learners to draw a picture of how the scent reached them. Discuss their responses and correct any misconceptions (see below).
- Use **PowerPoint 5.4**, slide 1, and ask the learners to identify what is happening in each of the pictures on the slide: water evaporates from wet clothes hanging in sunlight; ironing evaporates water from the clothes as they are ironed dry; a kettle boiling shows the formation of water vapour, the gaseous form of water.

Main activities

- Demonstrate water boiling and the evaporation that takes place, using the equipment available to you.
- Ask the learners to measure the initial volume of water using a measuring cylinder.
- For safety reasons, you will need to measure the volume of the residual water yourself (or ask an adult helper to do it). Discuss the difference in the volumes.
- During the demonstration, discuss what is happening in terms of the states of matter involved: the liquid (perfume or water) turns into a gas by evaporation.
- Revise the qualities of liquids: they take the shape of the container they are put into, they cannot be cut and they flow easily. In contrast, gases can be squashed and fill any space they occupy.
- Give out **Worksheet 5.4** and explain what the learners must do to complete it.

Some learners might think all states of matter can evaporate. Explain how evaporation only happens when a liquid changes into a gas.

Digging deeper

Support: Work with these learners in a small group to complete **Worksheet 5.4**.

Extension: Ask these learners to think of any other everyday examples of water evaporating and to write these on the back of their worksheet.

Wrapping up

- Check learners' understanding of what happens when liquids evaporate and become gases. Make sure they realise that, when water evaporates, it turns into water vapour.
- Ask learners to role-play being particles in a liquid, being heated up and evaporating.
- Talk through the answers to **Worksheet 5.4**.
- **Answers:**
  1 Evaporation happens when a **liquid** turns into a **gas**.
  2 See **PowerPoint 5.4**, slide 2, for a completed diagram of this.
  3 Heat or a higher temperature is needed to make a liquid turn into a gas.
  4 Water evaporates to become water vapour.
  5 Water vapour is also sometimes referred to as steam.

Assessment for learning

Ask the learners:
- *What is evaporation?*
- *What do you notice when steam is produced?*
- *How are the particles arranged in a liquid compared to the particles in a gas?*
- *How is the volume of water different after evaporation has happened?*

5.5 What is condensation?

Resources

PowerPoint 5.5; Worksheets 5.5a, 5.5b, 5.5c and 5.5d (Boost); heat source; container of water; tile or mirror; cling film/plastic wrap; beakers or containers for hot water; ice cubes; measuring cylinders

Starter activity

- Demonstrate boiling some water and allowing the water vapour to condense on a cold surface, such as a tile or a mirror.
- Ask the learners to explain what happened to the water vapour. (It turned back into liquid water.) Introduce the word 'condense'.
- Check learners' understanding from the previous lesson on evaporation to make sure they remember the following facts:
  - Water vapour is invisible.
  - Water evaporates from surfaces usually by the action of heat on them.
- Use **PowerPoint 5.5** to discuss some examples of condensation in everyday life. When water vapour, which is water in the gaseous state, comes into contact with a cold surface, the particles in the gas cool down and move closer together. This then turns into liquid water that can be seen on a window, for example. In other words, when water vapour condenses, it turns back into liquid water. Exhaled breath is warm, so it cools on contact with cold air, making condensation. Warm breath heats up the cold water vapour in the air and it is then seen as condensation.

Main activities

- Give out **Worksheets 5.5a** and **5.5b** to all learners except those who need an extension.
- Give **Worksheets 5.5c** and **5.5d** to learners who need an extension.
- Make sure that any hot water the learners use is not too hot for their hands.
- Put the learners in pairs or small groups, depending on the equipment and time available.

- Tell them to follow the instructions on their worksheets to set up and carry out the experiment, completing the responses as they work.
- Circulate around the room, observing, assisting and asking relevant questions as necessary to check learners' understanding and address any possible misconceptions.

Misconceptions

Some learners might think that when the water vapour condensed on the cold surface (the tile or mirror), the water vapour had soaked through it. Ensure learners understand that condensation is a change of state from gas to liquid and is caused by cooling.

Digging deeper

Support: Give these learners **Worksheets 5.5a** and **5.5b**. Organise these learners in a small group or mixed-ability groups so other learners can help them.

Extension: Give these learners **Worksheets 5.5c** and **5.5d**. Challenge them to measure the original volume of hot water used and the final volume remaining at the end of the experiment.

Wrapping up

- Discuss what happened and what the learners observed. (Condensation will have formed on the underside of the cling film/plastic wrap.) Note that, for **Worksheet 5.5d**, the volume of water could be the same or different, depending on conditions. If the beaker was completely sealed, the volume of water may remain the same as it is a closed system. However, the volume of water may be smaller as some will evaporate before condensing back into water droplets.
- Discuss why condensation occurs on cold taps in the bathroom or kitchen, or on cans of drink taken from the fridge. (This is because, when a gas touches a cold surface, it condenses back into a liquid.)

Assessment for learning

Ask the learners:
- *What did you observe?*
- *Why did this happen?*
- *Describe the droplets and what happened to them.*
- *What happens to water vapour when it hits a cold surface?*

5.6 Making solutions

Resources

PowerPoint 5.6; Worksheet 5.6 (Boost); water; fizzy lemonade; milk; white liquid paint; sugar; salt; flour; white powder paint (that can be mixed with water, i.e. not emulsion/wall paint); magnifying glasses; beakers; stirrers, spatulas or spoons

Starter activity

- Show the learners the selection of white and colourless solids and liquids available. Alternatively, refer to **PowerPoint 5.6** to talk about the different solids and liquids – as listed in the resources.
- Explain how they are all familiar everyday liquids and solids, but that they are **not** all safe to taste because they are not all foods or drinks.
- Ask the learners in pairs to form groups using the substances and identify the solids and liquids – without tasting any.
- Encourage them to use the magnifying glasses to help them make more careful observations of each solid or liquid.
- Discuss their groupings and their rationale for any groupings made. These reasons could include colour, solids or liquids, foods, drinks, or non-foods.
- Revise the properties of the solids presented (e.g. hard/powdery). Remind them that powders are made of small grains or particles of solid material.
- Revise the properties of liquids.

Main activities

- Explain to learners that, in this lesson, they will make some different solutions.
- Ask them what a solution is. (It is a solid dissolved in a liquid.) At this stage, the liquid mentioned is usually water.
- Ask them to suggest solutions that could be made from the solids and liquids available.
- Give out **Worksheet 5.6** to all learners. Explain that they need to follow the instructions and make the solutions.
- Discuss and compare their results.

Misconceptions

Some learners may think that substances disappear when they dissolve, i.e. they no longer exist or have gone somewhere because they cannot be seen. This can be shown to be untrue by demonstrating that the mass of a solution is equal to the combined weight of the solid and the solvent used to make the solution.

Digging deeper

Support: Limit the number of solutions for these learners to make up. Ask them to prepare fewer solutions than the other groups. Use water as the solvent for all the solutions you ask them to prepare. Work with them in a small group or offer individual support in completing **Worksheet 5.6**.

Extension: Ask these learners to find examples from everyday life where making solutions is involved; for example, in cooking, using dishwasher tablets or washing-up liquid, and some medicines (such as effervescent vitamins or dissolvable aspirin).

Wrapping up

- Discuss each solid and liquid used in turn.
- Introduce the terms 'solute' (the thing that dissolves) and 'solvent' (the liquid that the solute dissolves in).
- Compare how effective the solids and liquids used are as a solute or solvent in any solution made.
- Ask learners: *Which substances were soluble? Which substances did not dissolve?*

- Discuss what will happen to each of the solutions made if left. (The water will evaporate over time.)
- Keep the solutions to look at in the next lesson.

Assessment for learning

Ask the learners:
- *Which factors affect making a solution?*
- *Which liquid was the best solvent?*
- *What happens when a liquid evaporates from a solution?*
- *Name some coloured solids that dissolve in water to make solutions.*

5.7 Soluble or insoluble?

Resources

PowerPoint 5.7; Worksheet 5.7 (Boost); solutions prepared by the learners in the previous lesson; distilled water; beakers; stirrers; measuring spoons or spatulas; salt; sugar; sand; flour; instant coffee; measuring cylinders; scientific balance

Starter activity

- As a class, think back to the solutions made in the previous lesson. Look at them again now. Ask learners: *What has happened?* (Some of the water should have evaporated.)
- Ask the learners whether this is what they thought would happen. Can they explain why this has happened?
- Discuss what has happened to the water or liquid: *Where has it gone?* (It has not disappeared.)
- Remind the learners that this happens because of evaporation.

Main activities

- Use **PowerPoint 5.7** to recall the vocabulary for this lesson. 'Soluble' means a substance dissolves in a liquid. 'Insoluble' means the opposite; a substance does not dissolve in a liquid.

- Explain that, when a solid dissolves in water, it does not disappear; even if the solution is colourless, the solid is still there. The resulting solution is the solid mixed with water.
- Remind learners that it is not safe to taste liquids in science lessons, unless they are told by a teacher that the liquids are safe to drink.
- Explain that, in this lesson, they will make and separate some solutions.
- Give out **Worksheet 5.7** and talk through the instructions with them.
- Check (or ask them to share) their predictions before allowing them to make solutions.
- Discuss making this a fair test. To achieve this, learners will need to use equal amounts of water, equal amounts of substance and (if they suggest it) the same number of stirs each time.
- Ask them to think about the best equipment to use. Examples could include beakers, measuring cylinders, and spoons or spatulas. Consider the most suitable weight in grams of substance.
- Learners should work in pairs or groups, depending on the amount of equipment available.
- Allow them to choose from a limited range of suitable equipment.

Digging deeper

Support: Work in a small group with these learners or arrange for them to work in mixed-ability groups.

Extension: Ask these learners to rank the substances in order of solubility. *How can you compare them?* Perhaps compare the speed of dissolving under the same conditions: the only variable changed each time is the substance to be dissolved.

Wrapping up

- Compare and share results and findings.
- Discuss which substances are soluble and which are insoluble.
- Consider which substances will remain after evaporation has taken place.

Assessment for learning

Ask the learners:
- *How did you make this a fair test?*
- *Which substances do you predict will remain after evaporation?*
- *What remains after the liquid has evaporated?*
- *Did your results support your prediction(s)?*

5.8 Growing crystals

Resources

PowerPoint 5.8; Worksheet 5.8 (Boost); hand lenses or magnifying glasses; hot water; salt; sugar; washing soda; jewellery (with crystals); stirrers or glass rods; measuring cylinders; scientific balance; spatulas; beakers or glass jars; cotton thread; scissors; pencils; card; internet access or reference books on crystals; strong heat source

Starter activity

- Ask the learners to discuss in pairs: *What is a crystal?* (A crystal is a substance with a regular shape.)
- Diamonds could be considered the most beautiful crystals in the world. They have clear, flat faces that sparkle in the light.
- Ask learners, *Do you know of any crystals? Where would you find crystals at home? Do you know the shape of any crystals?*
- Use **PowerPoint 5.8** to look at a diamond and some salt and sugar crystals.
- Give learners an opportunity to observe some crystals using a hand lens or magnifying glass.
- Demonstrate how to use the hand lens, if necessary: hold the lens near to the eye and bring the object and the eye closer together. Good examples of crystals to use are salt or sugar.

Main activities

- Explain that most solids are made up of lots of crystals. We cannot usually see them because they are too small.
- Crystals can be many shapes and sizes. For example, salt crystals are cubic and sugar crystals are hexagonal prisms.

- Crystals for a particular substance are always the same shape; for example, salt crystals are always cubic in shape.
- Explain that, in today's lesson, the learners will grow crystals.
- Give out **Worksheet 5.8** and talk through the instructions with the learners.
- Demonstrate how to set up the experiment, with help from some of the learners.
- Note that, to grow the biggest crystal possible (using your demonstration set-up), learners must follow the instructions on **Worksheet 5.8**. After a day or two, small crystals should start appearing on the thread around the knot. Choose the best-looking crystal (square and big) and carefully knock off the smaller ones with the back of a knife, taking care not to cut the string.
- Replace the thread with the chosen crystal still attached in the solution.
- Do not add water to top up the solution, as this will dissolve the crystal.

Misconceptions

Some learners might think crystals are only found in jewellery. The activities in this lesson address this misconception.

Digging deeper

Support: Work with these learners in a small group to carry out the experiment.

Extension: Ask these learners to find examples of crystals from around the world. They should either carry out internet research or use the reference books provided. Gemstones (precious stones) are some of the best examples of crystals found around the world.

Wrapping up

- Demonstrate evaporation of water from a saturated salt solution. Use a strong heat source, such as a Bunsen burner or a saucepan on a cooker. (Rapid evaporation will leave behind small crystals.)
- Observe the small crystals when cool.
- Ask learners: *What do you think your crystals will look like?*

Assessment for learning

Ask the learners:
- *What is a saturated solution?*
- *What will happen to the water over time?*
- *What shape are sugar crystals?*
- *Why are the (salt) crystals prepared by the teacher small?*

5.9 What's in it?

Resources

PowerPoint 5.9; Worksheets 5.9a and 5.9b (Boost); prepared liquids: (A) saturated salt solution, (B) saturated sugar solution and (C) distilled water; general equipment, e.g. beakers, stirrers, evaporating dishes, heat sources (as required)

Starter activity

- Look at the crystals growing from the last lesson.
- Ask the learners to observe, compare and describe them.
- Ask them to draw a crystal if one is clearly visible.
- Set up a competition to grow the biggest crystal.
- Leave the crystals and look at them over an agreed period of time. Use **PowerPoint 5.9** to show some images of different crystals.
- Show the learners the three prepared liquids.
- Discuss how they are all the same in appearance.
- Explain that, in science, the learners will work with lots of colourless liquids but remind learners it is never a good idea to taste them (unless their teacher tells them they are safe to taste).
- Ask the learners to discuss in pairs what the liquids might be and how they could find out.
- Listen to their responses but only comment if what they are suggesting is unsafe or dangerous.

Main activities

- Explain that, in this lesson, the learners' challenge is to be scientific detectives. They will need to look for clues and identify each clear liquid.
- Give out **Worksheets 5.9a** and **5.9b** for the learners to complete.

- Discuss possible methods, useful equipment and how they will make sure they carry out a fair test.
- Explain that it is completely their decision which equipment and amounts of substances they use.
- They will only be able to carry out the experiment once you have approved their plans.
- Allow them to carry out the experiment and report back to the rest of the class at the end of the lesson.

Misconceptions

Some learners might think solutions are just water or that some different samples are the same solution. This activity will help them understand the difference between different colourless solutions.

Digging deeper

Support: Work with these learners in a small group; guide them through each stage of the planning process. Discuss choices carefully, making sure they agree on the equipment to use and how to carry out the experiment.

Extension: Give these learners some other solutions and ask them to identify the components. Try some coloured solutions, for example, fruit juice or powder paint in water. Ask them to predict and justify their predictions.

Wrapping up

- Ask the learners to identify the three liquids from the Main activities (not the Extension solutions).
- Agree the correct identifications. If they are unable to identify the liquids at this stage, let them know that they can, in this instance, taste them to check (with close adult supervision).
- Ask different groups or pairs of learners to describe their methods.
- Decide with the learners whether a fair test was carried out each time. Make suggestions to improve future testing if not.

Assessment for learning

Ask the learners:
- *What did you do?*
- *How did you decide what was in each liquid?*
- *What scientific process has happened to leave a solid behind?*
- *How did you make your test fair?*
- *Are all liquids solutions?*
- *What other solids might dissolve in water to make clear solutions?*

5 Unit assessment

Questions to ask

- *What happens when water evaporates?*
- *How is the process of condensation related to evaporation?*
- *What is temperature a measure of?*
- *What does a soluble solid mixed with water produce?*
- *What shape are salt crystals?*

Summative assessment activities

Observe the learners while they complete these activities. You will be able to quickly identify those who appear to be confident and those who might need additional support.

Evaporation or condensation?

This game assesses the learners' understanding of evaporation and condensation.

You will need:
A set of pre-prepared cards with pictures of everyday situations showing either evaporation or condensation, for example, a kettle boiling, clothes drying on a washing line, a steamed-up mirror, droplets of water on the outside of a glass containing an ice-cold drink

What to do
- Organise the learners into small groups, to take turns around the table.
- Place the cards randomly face down on the table. Ask one learner to choose a card and say whether it is an example of evaporation or condensation. They should then describe, using appropriate scientific vocabulary, exactly what is happening in the picture in terms of the process depicted.
- If they give a correct response, they should keep the card.
- Take turns until all the cards are used.
- The winner is the learner with the most cards in their possession at the end of the game.

Taking temperatures

This activity assesses the learners' understanding of temperature.

You will need:
A range of different liquids; stick thermometers with different temperature ranges on them

What to do
- Work with the learners either individually or in small groups.
- Give them the name of a liquid (for example, water at room temperature, a hot cup of coffee, water in a washing machine) or an object (for example, an ice cube, your body).
- Either ask them what the temperature is (water boils at 100°C and freezes at 0°C; human body temperature is 37°C) or ask them to show you the thermometer that they would choose to measure the temperature of the liquid or object, for example, room temperature.
- As an additional activity, the learners could check their predictions using thermometers.

Written assessment

Give learners time to complete **Worksheet 5.10**. The learners should work independently or with their usual in-class support.

Prior learning

Learners should be able to recall that gravity on Earth is a force that pulls towards the centre of the Earth. They should also be able to identify friction as a force created between surfaces when they move against each other and understand that this makes this movement more difficult. Some learners might be able to describe how smooth and rough surfaces can generate different amounts of friction.

Science in context

Lesson 6.2 provides an opportunity for learners to research good examples of surfaces to use for entry hall mats in a school.

6.1 Forces in action

Resources

PowerPoint 6.1; Worksheet 6.1 (Boost); trays and marbles; table tennis balls and drinking straws; soft modelling clay; marshmallows (or cotton wool balls) and elastic bands; poster paper

Starter activity

- Use **PowerPoint 6.1** to show this definition of a force: 'A force is a push or a pull'.
- A force can make an object:
  - start moving
  - change speed
  - change direction
  - change shape.
- Ask learners to think of an example of how they use a force to carry out each of the actions in the definition. Examples could include pulling a door open, pushing the pedals on a bicycle, hitting a ball or moulding clay.
- Collect their ideas and record them under the four statements on poster paper or on screen.
- Show the learners a marble on a tray.

- Demonstrate how you can make the marble start to move by tipping the tray, how you can make it change speed by tipping the tray further, and how you can change its direction by changing the angle of the tray.
- Ask the learners to think about this question: *How can we change the shape of the marble?* After they have suggested their ideas, explain that it will only change shape if you apply enough force to chip pieces off it!
- Show the learners how to record this information on **Worksheet 6.1**.

Main activities

- Set up a carousel of three activities (three different workstations) for the learners to explore as detailed on **Worksheet 6.1**.
- Allow ten minutes for the learners to work on each activity with a partner or in a small group.
- For each activity, they should explore how they make the object start to move and change direction, speed and shape.
- Ask the learners to record their observations on **Worksheet 6.1** as they explore.

Misconceptions

Some learners may believe that heavy objects fall faster because gravity pulls them down more strongly. This is not true: gravity acts equally on all objects but, on Earth, other factors (such as air resistance, upthrust) affect the rate of falling of an object.

Digging deeper

Support: Work with these learners in a small group to discuss their ideas.

Extension: Remove the images from **Worksheet 6.1** and ask these learners to think of other examples instead. Alternatively, ask them to complete **Worksheet 6.1** and then add any other examples on the back of the worksheet.

Wrapping up

- Talk through the answers to **Worksheet 6.1**. Ask some of the learners to share their explanations of the effect of the forces.

- Ask them to think about how they made the force bigger and the effect this had.

- Discuss other examples of where forces are acting; for example, trees blowing in the wind, pulling a suitcase, rolling out dough.

- Make sure they understand the concept that if an object starts to move or changes direction, speed or shape, then there must be a force that has caused this.

- Explain that pushes and pulls are examples of applied forces. When you push or pull an object, you are applying a force.

Assessment for learning

Ask the learners:

- *How did you describe the effect of each force?*
- *What is a force?*
- *Give an example of a force acting on an object to make it move.*
- *Give an example of a force acting on an object to make it change speed or direction.*
- *Give an example of a force acting on an object that makes it change shape.*

6.2 Measuring friction: an applied force

Resources

PowerPoint 6.2; Worksheet 6.2 (Boost); force meters; bricks or shoeboxes and masses; string; scissors; whiteboard or flipchart and markers; sticky notes; different surfaces; internet access or reference books about everyday uses of reducing friction

Starter activity

- Use **PowerPoint 6.2** to show a force meter; ask learners how to use it.
- Invite some learners to show how to use a force meter. This is good revision from Stage 3.
- Show the learners a heavy brick or a shoebox filled with masses. Tie the string around the brick or box and attach the force meter to it.
- Ask the learners to predict with talk partners the force in newtons that will be exerted if the brick (or box) is pulled along the surface of a table or desk.
- Record their predictions on sticky notes or a flipchart or whiteboard.
- Ask a learner to come forward and try it.
- Take the reading on the force meter and discuss how close their predictions were.

Main activities

- Remind the learners that friction is a force which acts between two surfaces (here we are using the brick/box and the tabletop).
- Compare the two different surfaces. Ask: *Are the two surfaces rough or smooth? Does this make a difference to the results?*
- Ask learners to find and name different surfaces around the room and around school (if permitted). (They may identify the floor of the classroom or corridor (wood/carpet/matting), the playground or the playing field.)
- Explain that, in this lesson, they will be able to plan and carry out an investigation to find out which surface has the least friction.
- Tell them they have to choose which surfaces they want to test.

- Discuss variables and fair testing. Remind them that only one variable should be changed each time (but don't tell them that this variable is the surface!).
- Organise learners into mixed-ability groups and give out **Worksheet 6.2** for them to plan and record their investigation.
- Check their method of recording results before they carry out the test.
- Go around the room helping, questioning and providing suggestions to make sure the learners are successful in their task.

Digging deeper

Support: Organise these learners into mixed-ability groups for this activity.

Extension: Ask these learners to find the best surface material for an entrance to school. Provide internet access or reference books to help them research this. Alternatively, set this as a homework activity for these learners.

Wrapping up

- Ask different groups of learners to share their conclusions. Do they agree?
- Discuss and decide on the best surface for reducing friction. Compare their measurements. (These will differ slightly according to the force meter they used.)
- Explain that friction is a force that can make moving objects slow down or stop. It reduces movement. It happens when two surfaces rub against each other.
- Friction is an example of an applied force as it is a pulling force. It is a force which is applied by one object (or person) on another object.

Assessment for learning

Ask the learners:
- *What is friction?*
- *Which surfaces did you test?*
- *Which surface had the least friction?*
- *Which surface had the most friction?*
- *How can we reduce friction?*

6.3 Sir Isaac Newton and gravity: another applied force

Resources

PowerPoint 6.3; Worksheet 6.3 (Boost); selection of different objects, such as a ball, a stone, an eraser, a feather, a coin; internet access or reference books about Newton and gravity

Starter activity

- This serves as good revision for Stage 3 work on gravity. Use **PowerPoint 6.3**, slide 1, to show images of objects falling. Ask learners: *What force causes this to happen?*

- Use **PowerPoint 6.3**, slide 2, which shows an image of Sir Isaac Newton and an apple. Ask learners whether they can recall the event that influenced his thoughts on gravity. Otherwise, re-tell the story to remind them … Briefly, it is said that, one day, when he was sitting underneath an apple tree, an apple fell on Newton's head! This made him think about why that happened. What caused the apple to fall? Thinking more about how all objects fall to the ground helped him to discover and name this force as gravity.

Main activities

- Demonstrate how all objects, when dropped, fall to the ground (or invite learners to come out and drop different objects).

- Give out **Worksheet 6.3** to all learners to give them some ideas about how they could structure their findings. However, encourage them to make a group resource such as a poster, factsheet or PowerPoint presentation. Give them free choice of how best to present their findings. Tell them presentations can be audio or video. Time will be needed to put up a display of their completed work and/or allow time for them to share their final presentations. This could take more than one lesson.

- Organise learners to work in pairs or small groups to carry out research about Sir Isaac Newton or to find experiments that demonstrate the

investigation of gravity. (Remind them of the bouncing balls activity from Stage 3.) Provide reference books and/or internet access for them to be able to do this.

Misconceptions

As mentioned in Lesson 6.1, some learners might think heavy objects fall faster because gravity pulls them down more strongly. Remind them that gravity acts equally on all objects. However, on Earth, other forces, such as air resistance and/or upthrust, will affect the rate of a falling object.

Digging deeper

Support: Organise these learners into mixed-ability groups for this activity so they can be supported by others. Carefully select reference materials and/or relevant websites appropriate for their reading level and amount of content.

Extension: Ask these learners to consider what implications Newton's scientific discoveries have for us today and will have in the future. (Responses will be open-ended depending on the current research they find.)

Wrapping up

- Ask different pairs or groups of learners to share one fact they have found out in this lesson (open-ended).

- Tell learners that they will be finding out later in this unit why it appears that gravity pulls more strongly on some objects than others.

- Gravity is another example of an applied force. It is a pulling force which is applied by the Earth's pull on objects.

Assessment for learning

Ask the learners:
- *Who discovered the force of gravity?*
- *Is the pull of gravity the same on all falling objects?*

6.4 Normal forces

Resources

PowerPoint 6.4; Worksheet 6.4 (Boost); wall space; selection of everyday classroom objects such as a desk, chair, book, pencil.

Starter activity

- Ask learners to recall what an applied force is (a push or a pull) and to name any examples (answers could include friction or gravity).
- Explain how, in this lesson, they will be finding out about another type of force: normal forces.
- Show **PowerPoint 6.4**, slide 1, for an example of a normal force. Use the image on this slide to describe how, when you push against a wall, there is another force pushing back at you. The force pushing back is the normal force.

Main activities

- Organise learners to work in pairs. Ask them to find a suitable space on a wall (indoors or outdoors), push against the wall and, with talk partners, describe what they can feel when they do this.
- Give out **Worksheet 6.4** to all learners to record their findings.
- Show **PowerPoint 6.4**, slides 2 and 3, to illustrate a pencil on a desk and someone sitting down on a sofa.
- Then ask them to observe a pencil placed on their desk. In pairs, learners should talk about what forces are acting on the pencil on the tabletop.
- Ask them then to think about the forces acting when they sit down on a comfortable sofa/couch or padded chair.

Misconceptions

Some learners might think an object at rest does not have any forces acting on it. Gravity is always pulling on an object, but it is balanced by the normal force from the object, which acts in the opposite direction.

Digging deeper

Support: Organise these learners into mixed-ability groups or work with them in a small group to discuss and record their observations and findings.

Extension: Ask these learners to find as many examples of normal forces as they can in the time available. Extra responses can be made on the back of the worksheet.

Wrapping up

- Talk through the answers to **Worksheet 6.4**.
- **Answers:**
  1 The wall does not move.
  2 The wall pushes back because forces always act in pairs.
  3 If the wall was not pushing back, you would fall down!
  4 The weight of the pencil is being acted on by the force of gravity and there is an opposing force, called a normal force, being exerted upwards by the table.
  5 When you sit on a comfortable sofa/couch, your mass is being acted on by the force of gravity. The opposing force from the sofa is acting upwards; this is the normal force.
- Ask learners to share other examples of normal forces they have found.
- Remind learners that a normal force is the 'pushing back' force.

Assessment for learning

Ask the learners:
- *What is a normal force?*
- *When you push against a wall, why does the wall not move?*
- *What forces are acting on an object at rest on a table?*

6.5 Air resistance

Resources

PowerPoint 6.5; Worksheet 6.5 (Boost); A4 (copy) paper; toy aeroplane or aeroplanes; sticky notes; internet access or reference books; digital camera

Starter activity

- Give each learner a piece of A4 (copy) paper. Ask them to drop it and observe how it falls.
- Now repeat the activity with the paper folded into four. In pairs, then small groups, then as a class, compare and discuss the difference.
- Ask the learners to screw the paper up into a ball and drop it again. Again, discuss and compare what happens.
- The learners should realise that changing the shape of the paper affects how it falls.
- Make a display of the various shapes of paper and ask different learners to write labels to describe the differences in how they fall through the air.

Main activities

- Explain that air resistance is another force, rather like friction. Air resistance is friction between air and something else.
- Use a toy aeroplane to demonstrate the forces operating around an aircraft when it is airborne.
- Use sticky labels or arrows to label the toy as 'thrust' when going forwards as it flies through the air and 'air resistance' pushing from the front to the back of the aeroplane. This is the pair of opposing forces affecting the plane.
- Use **PowerPoint 6.5** to talk about streamlining and how altering the shape of aeroplanes and cars can reduce air resistance and enable them to travel faster.

- Explain that you are going to have a competition to make paper aeroplanes to see which travels the furthest.
- Organise learners to work in pairs or small groups to research, make and test their paper aeroplanes within an agreed time limit.
- Provide them with reliable internet access or provide books and pictures with information about making paper aeroplanes.
- Give out **Worksheet 6.5** for the learners to record what they do.

Digging deeper

Support: Work in a small group with these learners, helping them to research the process and follow instructions for making a paper aeroplane.

Extension: Ask these learners to look at some aeroplanes throughout history. Challenge them to find out about their top speeds and make a list of pictures and facts to show the rest of the class.

Wrapping up

- Hold a 'flying competition' to find out which aeroplane flies the furthest. Discuss why the winning aeroplane was the winner – look at the shape and how streamlined it is.
- Remind the learners that streamlining reduces air resistance, so the aeroplane can 'cut through' the air more easily.

Assessment for learning

Ask the learners:
- *What is air resistance?*
- *How does the shape of an object change the way in which it is affected by air resistance?*
- *What is streamlining?*
- *How are friction and air resistance similar?*

6.6 Making parachutes

Resources

PowerPoint 6.6; Worksheets 6.6a and 6.6b (Boost); outdoor space; large pieces of paper (flipchart paper); electric fan/hairdryer (optional); string; scissors; modelling clay; squares of paper; timers; different materials for making canopies for the extension group

Starter activity

- Take the learners outside. Give each learner a piece of flipchart paper. Ask them to hold the paper in front of them and try to walk into the wind, or simply just to walk around. (If there is no wind outside, try using an electric fan or hairdryer indoors instead.)
- Discuss what it feels like. Explain that the force the learners can feel pushing against them is air resistance.

Main activities

- Return to the classroom. Use **PowerPoint 6.6** to show more examples of air resistance.
- Hand out the string, scissors, modelling clay and squares of paper to the learners, who should work in pairs or small groups.
- Tell learners how to make a paper parachute.
- Give clear instructions on how to attach string to the corners of the canopy and how to attach the mass of modelling clay.
- Demonstrate how to do this as you give the instructions so that the learners can copy what you are doing, then allow learners to make their own parachutes.
- Try out several of these parachutes and time how long it takes for them to reach the ground from the time they were released into the air.
- Ask the learners to predict whether the parachutes should take more time, less time or the same amount of time to fall from the same height. (They should take the same amount of time if they are identical.)
- Ask some of the learners to time the fall and the other learners to record the times.

- Discuss the results and any differences. Use this to highlight the importance of fair testing and that human error can sometimes have an effect.
- Ask: *Did you follow the instructions precisely?*
- Think about repeating results to get an average time to obtain more reliable results.
- Ask the learners to predict how the size of a parachute will affect the rate of fall.
- Give out **Worksheets 6.6a** and **6.6b** for the learners to record their investigation.
- Organise them into mixed-ability groups to carry out the activity and complete **Worksheets 6.6a** and **6.6b**.

Digging deeper

Support: Organise these learners into mixed-ability groups to carry out the parachute investigation.

Extension: Ask these learners to further investigate whether the parachute material makes any difference to the speed of falling. Provide some different materials to these learners for their investigation.

Wrapping up

- Invite groups in turn to present their findings to the rest of the class.
- Ask questions to compare similarities and differences in their results.
- Predict the rate of fall of a parachute twice the size of the largest one used in the activity. If there is time, try this out.

Assessment for learning

Ask the learners:
- *Which force acts downwards for a parachute?*
- *What is the opposing, upwards force?*
- *Which size of parachute fell the fastest?*
- *Which parachute took the longest time to land?*
- *Why did this happen?*
- *How does the size of the parachute affect the rate of fall?*

6.7 Water resistance

Resources

PowerPoint 6.7; Worksheets 6.7a and 6.7b (Boost); large measuring cylinders; thick, colourless glue or similar thick liquid; soft modelling clay; stopwatches or timers

Starter activity

- Recap the learners' understanding of friction as a force that slows things down.

- Ask the learners to think about walking through the water in a swimming pool: *Is it easy or difficult?* Explain that we find it hard to walk through water because we have to push through the water. The water slows us down.

- Use **PowerPoint 6.7**, which shows a fish swimming in water. Ask: *Why do you think fish can swim easily through the water?* Talk about how the shape of the fish (or any object) affects how easily it can move through the water.

- Explain how, in this lesson, they are going to investigate how shape affects how easily something can move through a liquid.

Main activities

- Fill a large measuring cylinder with a thick, colourless liquid.

- Drop a small piece of modelling clay into the liquid and use a stopwatch or timer to time how long it takes to reach the bottom of the measuring cylinder.

- In pairs or small groups, give learners a piece of soft modelling clay. Tell them to make it into six balls of modelling clay, each the same size. Then tell them to make each ball into a different shape.

- Ask them to record the shapes they have made on **Worksheet 6.7a** and put them in order according to how easily they think each shape will move through the liquid.

- Tell learners to carry out the test by dropping each shape in turn into the liquid and timing how long it takes to reach the bottom using a stopwatch or timer.

- Make sure they record their results on **Worksheet 6.7a**.

- If it is not possible for the learners to carry out this investigation, there is a set of results provided on **Worksheet 6.7b**. This can be used for interpretation of data.

Digging deeper

Support: Give these learners **Worksheet 6.7a** with some shapes already drawn on it.

Extension: Ask these learners to think of objects that need to move through the water easily and how they are shaped to do this; for example, boats, submarines and fish. Allow them to try to make these shapes and test their predictions.

Wrapping up

- Ask the learners which shapes they found moved most easily through the water: *What do these shapes have in common?*

- Remind learners of the shapes that did not move easily through the water because they were being slowed down by a force. This force is known as 'water resistance' and it resists or prevents things moving easily through water.

Assessment for learning

Ask the learners:
- *What variable did you change in your investigation?*
- *What variables did you keep the same?*
- *How easy was it to time how long the shape took to reach the bottom?*
- *Did you predict correctly which shapes moved through the liquid most easily?*
- *Why did we use a thick, clear liquid instead of water for this investigation?*

6.8 Force diagrams

Resources

PowerPoint 6.8; Worksheets 6.8a and 6.8b (Boost); colouring pencils

Starter activity

- Ask the learners to discuss with their talk partners: *Which direction does gravity act in? How do you know?*
- Remind the learners that in Stage 3 they learnt about forces being pushes and pulls.

Main activities

- Use **PowerPoint 6.8** to talk about some different forces acting on objects. (These are the same objects that are on **Worksheet 6.8a**.)
- For each picture, discuss which forces are in action and what happens when a force is applied.
- Discuss the fact that there may be more than one force acting on an object.
- Describe gravity as a pulling force. Ask: *Which pictures show objects being pulled to Earth?* Remind them that gravity pulls things down to Earth and that this is why some things fall down or sink in water.
- Explain that the direction in which forces act is sometimes shown in force diagrams by arrows: the bigger the force, the bigger the arrow. Demonstrate this, using the images on **PowerPoint 6.8**.
- Give out **Worksheet 6.8a** to all learners to draw on directional arrows of the main forces acting in the pictures and to name each force.
- Give **Worksheet 6.8b** to all learners who do **not** need support.

Misconceptions

Some learners might think that an object at rest has no forces acting on it. Gravity is always acting on an object, but it is balanced by any normal force from the surface acting in the opposite direction.

Support learners in drawing force diagrams according to convention: that is, with arrows in the correct place, size and direction. Ask them to name the force and draw directional arrows for the direction in which it is acting.

Digging deeper

Support: Give these learners **Worksheet 6.8a** only. Help them by discussing the pictures before they draw the arrows.

Extension: Ask these learners to label as many different forces as possible in each picture, using different colours for different forces and writing a key to explain the colours.

Wrapping up

- Discuss the learners' responses. Revise the word 'upthrust' and describe it as a push that opposes gravity. Explain that this is the reason that some things float on water: the downard pull of gravity is balanced by the upward-acting force of upthrust.
- Ask learners why they think some objects sink in water, due to the effect of forces acting on them. Just listen to their ideas at this stage; this will be covered in more detail in Stage 6.
- Remind them that air resistance is the force that slows down a parachute falling to Earth. Gravity pulls the parachute down to Earth, but air resistance is an upward force that pushes against the force of gravity.

Assessment for learning

Ask the learners:
- *What kind of a force is gravity?*
- *Why do some things float?*
- *Which force balances gravity so that things float?*
- *What does air resistance do?*
- *What is a normal force?*

6 Unit assessment

Questions to ask

- *Give an example of a force acting on an object that makes it change shape.*
- *How can we reduce friction?*
- *Is the pull of gravity the same on all falling objects?*

- *What is air resistance?*
- *Which force balances gravity to make things float?*

Summative assessment activities

Observe the learners while they complete these activities. You will be able to quickly identify those who appear to be confident and those who might need additional support.

Forces in action

This activity assesses the learners' ability to identify forces and show their understanding of what effect forces can have on objects.

You will need:

A selection of objects including a ball, a toy vehicle, a glass marble, modelling clay, an elastic band

What to do

- Ask a learner to choose an object or different objects and show you how, by applying different forces, the object(s) can be made to:
  - start moving
  - change speed
  - change direction
  - change shape.
- Ask what kind of force – push or pull – has been applied to the object(s).
- Ask them to name any specific forces they recognise while doing this.
- Record their responses; perhaps use a checklist for quick reference to what they have remembered.

Force diagrams

You will need:

A selection of objects from around the classroom; a set of arrow cards; a set of labels with the words 'friction', 'upthrust', 'air resistance', 'gravity', 'water resistance'

What to do

- Set up an object, such as a book on a table. Ask the learner to use the arrow cards and labels and place them around the object to show the name and direction of the forces acting on that object.
- Repeat this activity several times with different objects to demonstrate different forces in action.
- Record their responses or take photographic evidence to note their understanding and/or any misconceptions.

Written assessment

Distribute **Worksheet 6.9**. The learners should work independently or with their usual in-class support.

Unit 7   Sound

Prior learning

Learners should be able to identify different sources of sound; for instance, a bell ringing or a bird chirping. They should also be able to recall how, as sound travels further away from a sound source, it gets quieter.

Science in context

Lesson 7.2 provides an opportunity for learners to find out about how drums work.

7.1 Vibrations

Resources

PowerPoint 7.1; Worksheet 7.1 (Boost); tuning forks; table tennis (ping pong) ball with cotton thread attached using sticky tape; cup or small bowl of water; drum; drumsticks; rice; flexible plastic ruler; large, thick elastic band; box without a lid (e.g. cardboard shoe box)

Starter activity

- Ask the learners to place their fingers on their throat and hum a tune. Ask: *What can you feel?* They should be able to feel their throat moving as they make a sound.
- Explain that the movement of their vocal cords in their throat is called a vibration. Explain that sounds are produced when something vibrates.
- Therefore, for every sound, there is a movement that creates the sound.
- Show the learners a tuning fork. Strike the tuning fork on the table and listen to the note produced. Do this several times, taking it around the room so that all the learners can hear it. Ask: *How can you describe the sound this tuning fork makes?* (high, quiet and continuous)
- Again strike the tuning fork and take it around the classroom, this time asking the learners to look closely to see if they can see the movement that is producing the sound.

- Explain that, if you look very closely, the ends of the tuning fork appear to be blurred. This is because they are moving backwards and forwards very quickly indeed to produce vibrations, which make the sound you can hear.
- Alternatively, use **PowerPoint 7.1** to show how a tuning fork works. The video shows the tines (prongs) on a tuning fork vibrating after it has been hit.

Main activities

- Set up a carousel (five different workstations for learners to circulate through) of the five activities listed on **Worksheet 7.1**.
- Organise learners to work in pairs or small groups so they can discuss their observations.
- Explain to the learners that they need to visit each activity in turn, follow the instructions and write their responses on **Worksheet 7.1**.

Misconceptions

Some learners might think sound moves between particles. In fact, particles move and transfer energy in a chain to create a sound wave. This will be studied in greater detail in later stages.

Digging deeper

Support: Give these learners the option to draw labelled diagrams to show their observations instead of providing written answers.

Extension: Check that these learners can use the correct scientific vocabulary in their explanations; for example, 'vibrates', 'vibrations', 'vibrating'.

Wrapping up

- Talk through the answers to **Worksheet 7.1**.
- **Answers:**
  - When the tuning fork touches the suspended table tennis ball, the table tennis ball moves away from it. This is because it is very light and the vibrations push it away through the air.

- On the surface of the water, ripples are made because vibrations from the tuning fork are transferred to the water and travel through it, creating ripples on the surface.

- When you pluck an elastic band, it stretches and, when it is released, it makes a sound. Different thicknesses of elastic band produce different sounds when plucked because they vibrate more or less slowly.

- The rice on the drum bounces or dances as the drum skin vibrates after it has been hit. The grains are shaken about because they are small and light.

- The ruler on the edge of the table 'twangs' and makes a sound. The twanging sound is produced by the end of the ruler vibrating.

- Remind the learners that sounds are caused by something vibrating, for example, the tines of the tuning fork.

- Vibrations are often too small to see but we can observe the effects they create.

Assessment for learning

Ask the learners:
- *Describe how a sound is made.*
- *What is a vibration?*
- *Give an example of when we can see vibrations.*

7.2 Investigating musical instruments

Resources

PowerPoint 7.2; Worksheets 7.2a (pre-prepared) and 7.2b; flashcards (Boost); sticky notes; internet access; range of musical instruments; drums and different types of beaters for the extension activity

Starter activity

- Organise learners into pairs or small groups and then give each group the images of musical instruments from **Worksheet 7.2a** cut out as cards and placed in a pile.
- Ask learners: *What do these images show?* Give them a few minutes to look at all the images on the cards. (They are all musical instruments.)
- Discuss any instruments that are unfamiliar to them.
- Ask the learners to think of a criterion for sorting these instruments into two groups; for example, 'instruments that are made mostly of wood'/'instruments not made mostly of wood'. They should write the criteria on sticky notes.
- Give learners five to ten minutes to try as many different ways of sorting as they can.
- Finally, ask them to sort the instruments according to how they think they are played. They might suggest groupings such as blow, hit and pluck. Ask learners which group the guiro would fit into or whether it is in a group of its own. Why would this be?

Main activities

- Show **PowerPoint 7.2**, which has a link to a clip of a young boy playing a drum kit.
- Ask the learners to explain how they know he is playing the drum. They may answer that they can see him hitting it and they can hear the sound.
- Ask: *How do we hear the sound?* (It travels from the instrument to our ears through the air.)

- Ask: *Do all drums make the same sound? How might they sound different?*
- Give the learners time to explore making sounds using the different instruments available.
- Give each learner **Worksheet 7.2b** on which to record their ideas about how to play the instruments and how to describe the sounds they make.

Digging deeper

Support: Give additional support to these learners by giving them the set of flashcards to help them describe the sounds.

Extension: Make the activity more challenging for these learners by providing them with just drums and different types of beaters. They can explore how the different beaters produce different sounds. If there is time, ask them to prepare a performance to give to the rest of the class at the end of the lesson.

Wrapping up

- Describe how the term 'volume' relates to how loud or quiet a sound is.
- Remind the learners that the instruments make sounds that we can hear because sound travels through the air to our ears.
- Invite the learners who completed the extension activity to perform their drumming music.

Assessment for learning

Ask the learners:
- *In how many different ways did you sort the instrument cards? Give me some examples of the criteria you used.*
- *Describe how to make a sound with* [name of musical instrument].
- *Explain how you know an instrument is being played.*
- *How would you describe the sounds made by the different instruments you looked at?*

7.3 Making shakers

Resources

PowerPoint 7.3; Worksheets 7.3a, 7.3b and 7.3c (Boost); different-sized containers, with lids, made of different materials to make shakers, including plastic bottles, metal food tins and cardboard boxes; small items to put in the shakers, for example, rice, dried pasta shapes, peppercorns, marbles, cotton wool balls; sticky tape; datalogger or sound meter (if available) connected to a computer; whiteboard or flipchart and markers; paper

Starter activity

- Explain to the learners that you would like to make a loud shaker that could be used in the playground to signal when break time is over.
- Give out **Worksheet 7.3a** to all learners. Ask them to work with talk partners and discuss whether these variables are important or not. Ask: *If you were able to choose any material at all to make your shaker, what would you choose?*
- Ask the learners to complete **Worksheet 7.3a** on their own.

Main activities

- Display **PowerPoint 7.3**, which shows some different kinds of shakers. Discuss as a class which shaker they think would make the loudest noise.
- Show the learners the datalogger or sound meter (if available) and explain that it can be used to measure sound levels.
- If possible, connect it to a computer so that the learners can observe how the reading changes as they make more or less noise.
- Explain that the units used for measuring sound levels are called decibels.
- Show the learners the resources available.
- In pairs, ask learners to make a shaker that they think will produce the loudest possible sound.

- When each pair has made a shaker, ask a few to come to the front, shake their shaker and take a reading using the datalogger.
- As each shaker is played, take one reading and record this on a large table drawn on the whiteboard or flipchart.
- Repeat the test for each shaker. (The two readings will probably be slightly different due to the variation in how the shaker is being shaken.)
- Ask: *How do we know which result is correct?* Repeat the reading several times so that you can see what the range is; the range of one shaker might be between 62 and 86 decibels, for example.
- Organise the learners into groups to measure the sound produced by their shakers. Give out **Worksheet 7.3b** for them to record their results.

Digging deeper

Support: Support these learners to complete the table on **Worksheet 7.3b**. These learners could use the graphs produced by the datalogger to support them with answering the questions.

Extension: Ask these learners to construct their own bar chart using **Worksheet 7.3c**. Ask them to use the bar chart to present their own results.

Wrapping up

- Ask the learners to think about how we use the datalogger to get reliable readings.
- Make sure learners understand that they need to keep the distance between the source and datalogger the same for each test.
- As a class, discuss why it was a good idea to take repeat readings. Explain how it is important to take repeated readings if you think the results might change if you were to do it again. If an experiment can be repeated with similar results, this ensures that the experimental conditions are reliable. The repeat readings also showed the range of volume the shaker could make, depending on how it was shaken.

- **Answers:**
  - **Worksheet 7.3a:** open-ended responses, depending on the resources available to make the shakers with.
  - **Worksheets 7.3b** and **7.3c:** open-ended responses, depending on the datalogger or sound meter used.

Assessment for learning

Ask the learners:
- *What units do we measure sound in?*
- *How did you measure the sound level?*
- *Explain why you sometimes need to take repeat readings.* (see notes in Wrapping up section above)

7.4 Making bangers

Resources

PowerPoint 7.4; Worksheets 7.4a, 7.4b and 7.4c (Boost); datalogger (if available); paper of different sizes (A4/copy paper, i.e. 210 × 297 mm, to large newspaper) and thicknesses; graph paper

Starter activity

- Display **PowerPoint 7.4**, which shows how to make a paper banger. Note: this video shows this using a larger piece of paper (A3 or 297 × 420 mm) but the process is the same for all sizes of paper.
- Then, show the learners how to make a banger by folding paper, following the instructions on **Worksheets 7.4a** and **7.4b**.
- Most of the folds are valley folds, but the fold for instruction 9 is a mountain fold:

valley fold   mountain fold

- Show the learners how to hold the banger by the corner and make it bang by bringing it down really fast using your whole arm.
- Show the learners the banger so that they can see how it has changed: a flap that was inside the banger is now on the outside.
- With talk partners, ask them to discuss the question: *How was the sound made?* They should be able to work out that air forces the inside flap out suddenly. This makes the air around the flap vibrate, which creates the bang.

Main activities

- Give learners a piece of A4/copy paper to make a banger following the instructions on **Worksheets 7.4a** and **7.4b**.
- Give them time to practise using the banger.
- With talk partners, ask learners to discuss this question: *Does the banger get louder or quieter when you use it again?*

- Ask them to record their prediction on **Worksheet 7.4c**, reminding them that they should give a reason for their prediction.
- Ask the class: *How could you test this?* The easiest way would be to make one new banger and test it, recording the sound with a datalogger (sound level meter).
- Give each group a datalogger to carry out the investigation, recording their results on **Worksheet 7.4c**. Alternatively, give them access to any dataloggers available. If dataloggers are not available, they could do the activity and rank the loudness (volume) according to what they hear. (This will produce very varied results, depending on the learners' hearing abilities.)

Digging deeper

Support: Make the bangers with these learners, carrying out one step at a time together.

Extension: Ask these learners to draw a bar chart showing their results.

Wrapping up

- Ask each of the groups: *Was there a pattern in your results? If so, did your results show that the bangers got better or worse?* (The results are likely to be inconclusive.) Ask the learners to think about how they could improve the investigation. (Suggestions could include testing more bangers or being in separate rooms so the measurements are not affected by the other groups.)
- **Answers:** open-ended; in general, the banger should become less loud the more it is used.

Assessment for learning

Ask the learners:
- *What units are used when measuring sound levels?* (decibels)
- *How did you measure the sound level?*
- *Did your results support your prediction?*

7.5 Measuring sounds we can make

Resources

PowerPoint 7.5; Worksheet 7.5 (Boost); whiteboard or flipchart and markers; datalogger or sound level meter connected to a computer. Set these up in a place which is relatively soundproof or as far away from others as possible as there will be a lot of noise!

Starter activity

- With talk partners, ask learners to think about any sound they could make if they wanted to attract someone's attention, for example, if they were stuck up a tree. Listen for suggestions such as shouting, clapping, shaking the tree, whistling (if this is culturally acceptable), singing or humming. Write any suggestions on the flipchart or whiteboard so everyone can see them.
- **PowerPoint 7.5** shows a range of different sounds humans can make.
- As a class, discuss this question: *Which of your suggestions do you think is the loudest? How can we test this?* (They might suggest comparing the sounds or measuring how far away you can be and still hear the sound. Alternatively, if they have been using sound meters and dataloggers previously in this unit, they might suggest using these again.)

Main activities

- Explain that, as a class, they will be investigating the level of sound produced by some of the different noises they can make.
- Give **Worksheet 7.5** to all learners.

- Before starting the investigation, explain to learners that they will be asked to make each sound as loudly as possible for a short period of time. When a reading of the sound level is obtained, they will need to stop immediately.
- You should agree a visual signal so they know when to stop; for example, raising your hand.
- Practise starting and stopping a noise using the visual signal.
- Carry out the investigation together, asking the learners to record their results on **Worksheet 7.5** and then answer the questions on the worksheet.

Digging deeper

Support: Support these learners in completing the table on **Worksheet 7.5**. They could use the graphs produced by the datalogger to support them with answering the questions.

Extension: Ask these learners to draw their own bar chart to present their results.

Wrapping up

- Remind learners that decibels are the units used for measuring sound level.
- Ask learners which sound was the loudest.
- All answers to the questions on the worksheet will be open-ended responses.

Assessment for learning

Ask the learners:
- *How did you know which sound you made was the loudest?*

7.6 Changing sounds

Resources

PowerPoint 7.6; Worksheet 7.6 (Boost); internet access; glass bottle; jugs of water; pencils; rulers; drinking straws; scissors; box without lid; elastic bands of different thicknesses; balloon; drum; different types of drumsticks; stringed instrument

Take care when using glass bottles. If there are any breakages, make sure learners know to ask an adult to clear up any broken glass.

Starter activity

- Show the learners a drum and ask how it can be played in different ways. (They might suggest playing it with their hands or with a stick or beater (drumstick), hitting it harder or softer.)
- Demonstrate their ideas to them or ask volunteer learners to come and show what they mean.
- Ask the volunteers or the rest of the class to describe how this changes the sound produced. (It changes the volume if hit harder or softer.)
- Then ask: *If we are playing an instrument, what else do we want to change about the sound we produce?* (We may also want to change the pitch of the note; that is, how high or low the note is.)
- Use **PowerPoint 7.6**, slide 1, which explains how you can change the pitch of a drum.
- Discuss with the class the two ways in which the pitch of the drum note can be changed. (changing the size of the drum (and so the volume of air inside it) and the tightness of the skin)

Main activities

- Using the stringed instrument available, demonstrate how when you pluck a string gently, it produces a quiet sound. Then demonstrate how to make it louder by plucking the string harder. Explain that this is the volume of a sound.
- Make sure learners understand how large vibrations create loud sounds and small vibrations produce quieter sounds.
- Discuss with the class the fact that fast vibrations produce high-pitched sounds and slower vibrations produce lower-pitched sounds.
- Ask the learners to make one of their fingers vibrate by wiggling it.

- Repeat, but this time ask learners to wiggle their arm. Ask: *Which is easiest to vibrate more quickly: your finger or your arm?*
- Explain how fast vibrations are caused by less material being vibrated. A small drum and shorter strings on musical instruments will produce higher notes.
- Give each learner **Worksheet 7.6**. Organise the class into small groups or pairs and set up the workstations. Each group should then visit the workstations to carry out each of the activities on **Worksheet 7.6**.
- Tell them these activities will allow them to explore what happens when they change the pitch and volume of different 'instruments'.
- If there is time, show the YouTube clip on **PowerPoint 7.6**, slide 2, which illustrates some of the concepts about sound, including volume and pitch.

Digging deeper

Support: Work with these learners in a small group as they explore each activity to help them identify which material is vibrating.

Extension: Ask these learners to work out and explain why the pitch changes.

Wrapping up

- As a class, discuss how the learners changed the volume and the pitch of each 'instrument' at each workstation.
- Point out the different effects of adding water to the bottle when you blow over the top of the bottle (the note becomes higher) and when you tap it (the note becomes lower).
- **Answers: Worksheet 7.6** (L–R, top to bottom)
  - Tapping a bottle of water with a pencil: change the volume by hitting it harder or softer; change the pitch by changing the amount of water in the bottle.
  - Blowing across the top of a bottle of water: change the volume by blowing harder or more gently; change the pitch by changing the amount of water in the bottle.
  - Twanging a ruler: change the volume by hitting it with more or less force; change the pitch by making the length of ruler hanging over the edge of the desk shorter.

- Blowing through a flattened straw: change the volume by blowing harder; change the pitch by shortening the length of the straw (by cutting it with scissors).
- Plucking an elastic band: change the volume by plucking the elastic band harder or more gently; change the pitch by using different thicknesses of elastic bands.
- Letting air out of a balloon: change the volume when letting air out of the balloon by squeezing the balloon; change the pitch by squeezing the neck of the balloon tighter.

Assessment for learning

Ask the learners:
- *How did you change the volume of each sound?*
- *How did you change the pitch of the sound in [name a particular activity]?*
- *Explain why the pitch changed each time.*

7 Unit assessment

Questions to ask

- *How are sounds made?*
- *What is a vibration?*
- *How do sounds travel to your ear?*
- *What is volume?*

- *What is pitch?*
- *Describe how to change the pitch of a musical instrument.*
- *How can you change the volume of different musical instruments?*

Summative assessment activities

Changing pitch and volume

This game provides an opportunity for the learners to talk about how the pitch and volume of sounds are changed.

You will need:
A guitar or similar

What to do

- Show the learners the guitar and ask them to discuss how they could change the volume (strumming harder or softer).
- Ask the learners to explain how the pitch of a guitar can be changed (changing the length of the string by pressing down on it at various points along the fretboard). They can draw diagrams to help their explanations if necessary.

Playing a tune

This activity encourages the learners to think about how to change the pitch of a note.

You will need:
Glass bottles; water; pencils

Take care when using glass bottles. If there are any breakages, make sure learners know to ask an adult to clear up any broken glass.

What to do

- Divide the learners into small groups and provide each group with eight glass bottles.
- Ask them to tune the bottles to create different notes by filling them to different levels with water. Ask the learners to explain how they are

changing the pitch of the notes produced by the different bottles.

- Challenge them to play a familiar tune using the different notes from the bottles.

Noisy classroom

This activity assesses how well the learners can interpret and explain graphs.

You will need:
A datalogger

What to do

- Set the datalogger up in the classroom and leave it recording for 24 hours, for example from 8 a.m. on one day to 8 a.m. the following day.
- Print out the graph from the datalogger for each learner. Point out the times on the graph when the classroom was noisy and when it was quiet.
- Ask questions and challenge the learners to annotate the graph to explain the shape of it; for example: *What was happening when the classroom was the noisiest? When was it the quietest? Why was that?*

Written assessment

Give learners time to complete **Worksheet 7.7**. The learners should work independently or with their usual in-class support.

Prior learning

Learners should be able to recall the fact that each end of a magnet is called a pole: the north and south poles. They should also be able to recall and use the terms 'attract' and 'repel' appropriately. Some learners might remember which materials in general are magnetic and which are non-magnetic.

Science in context

Lesson 8.4 provides an opportunity for some learners to research uses of strong magnets in everyday life.

8.1 Magnets and magnetic materials

Resources

PowerPoint 8.1; Worksheets 8.1a and 8.1b (Boost); range of different types of magnets (as available) such as bar magnets, horseshoe magnets, circular magnets, ring magnets; selection of different materials, both magnetic and non-magnetic, such as steel paper clips, paper, fabric, iron nails, steel spoons, wooden or plastic rulers

Starter activity

- Use **PowerPoint 8.1**, slide 1, to show a range of different types of magnet. This serves as revision of prior knowledge, to find out what learners have remembered about magnets from Stage 3. Ask learners to name any of the types of magnet.
- Use **PowerPoint 8.1**, slide 2, to show different types of materials, both magnetic and non-magnetic. Ask: *Which of these materials would be attracted to a magnet? Why?* Do not correct learners' ideas. The lesson will help them to revise basic concepts about magnetism.

Main activities

- Explain to learners that, in this lesson, they will be using magnets to remind themselves about properties of magnets and magnetic materials.
- Show them the range of magnets available for them to work with.
- Organise learners into pairs or small groups, depending on how many magnets and materials you have.
- Give **Worksheet 8.1a** to learners who need support and **Worksheet 8.1b** to all other learners to record their responses.
- Give learners time to explore using different magnets and materials to find out some properties of magnets and what kinds of materials they attract.

Misconceptions

Some learners might think magnetism can be passed from a magnet to a material and can then turn that material into a magnet. Explain how magnetism is a physical force, which attracts magnetic materials, but does not create magnets in the materials that are attracted to it.

Digging deeper

Support: Give these learners **Worksheet 8.1a** to complete. Organise them into mixed-ability pairs or small groups for peer support. Alternatively, work with them in a small group to support their completion of **Worksheet 8.1a**.

Extension: Give these learners **Worksheet 8.1b** to complete. This allows more open-ended, less-scaffolded opportunities for them to record their findings.

Wrapping up

- Talk through the answers to **Worksheets 8.1a** and **8.1b**.
- **Answers: Worksheet 8.1a**
  1 a) circular magnet
    b) ring magnet
    c) horseshoe magnet
    d) bar magnet
  2 open-ended responses
  3 magnet, magnetism, magnetic, attract(ion), repel, pole(s) (Accept in any order. This is not an exhaustive list. Refer also to the vocabulary list for this lesson. Accept any scientifically correct responses.)
- **Answers: Worksheet 8.1b**
  1 Look for responses including the types of magnets used in the lesson, but, perhaps also examples from everyday life, such as fridge magnets, magnetic toys, etc.

  2 Look for a range of recording methods, for example, tables, charts, mind maps, drawings, written responses.

  3 A magnet is a piece of equipment that can attract some materials. Magnetic materials are attracted to a magnet. (Accept examples if given, for example, steel or iron objects or metals are magnetic materials.)
- Make sure learners can use the word 'attract' appropriately and know what it means. Model correct use of the scientific vocabulary in this and every lesson.

Assessment for learning

Ask the learners:
- *Name some different types of magnet.*
- *Name a magnetic material you have found in this lesson.*
- *What is the difference between a magnet and a magnetic material?*

8.2 Magnetic poles and magnetic fields

Note: This material could be covered in two lessons, depending on the time available, with one lesson on magnetic poles and the other on magnetic fields.

Resources

PowerPoint 8.2, Worksheets 8.2a and 8.2b (Boost); pairs of bar magnets; iron filings in a shaker container (if their use is permitted); large sheets of paper; shrink wrap (optional); different types of magnets for extension activity

Starter activity

- Display **PowerPoint 8.2**, slide 1, which shows a bar magnet. As a class, talk about the bar magnet: learners should recall the terms 'north pole' and 'south pole'. Introduce the term 'magnetic pole'.
- Explain to learners how, in this lesson, they will revise how magnets work.
- Show **PowerPoint 8.2**, slide 2, which lists some rules about handling magnets safely.

Main activities

- Give **Worksheet 8.2a** to learners who need support and **Worksheet 8.2b** to all other learners.
- Organise the class into small groups and give each group a pair of bar magnets. Ask them to investigate the different situations shown on their worksheets and to record their individual responses to Questions 1 and 2.
- Demonstrate how to show the magnetic field around a bar magnet. Either place a bar magnet under a piece of paper and note which pole is at each end, or wrap a bar magnet in shrink wrap and place it on top of a large piece of paper. (This makes it easier to remove the iron filings from the magnet later.) Sprinkle iron filings around the magnet and watch as the patterns appear.
- Display **PowerPoint 8.2**, slide 3, which shows a labelled diagram of the magnetic field around a bar magnet. Describe the direction of the arrows drawn from north to south poles.

- Ask learners to carry out this activity themselves in pairs or small groups (if the use of iron filings by Stage 5 learners is permitted in your school). Then they should complete their worksheet to show what they find. Alternatively, if they are not allowed to use iron filings, they can complete the worksheet after your demonstration.

Misconceptions

Some learners might think magnets 'stick' to each other when they attract. Demonstrate that magnets are not sticky by showing learners how a magnet can still be attracted to another magnet even if a sheet of paper is placed in between them.

Digging deeper

Support: Give these learners **Worksheet 8.2a**. Either work with them in a small group or allow them to work in mixed-ability groups with peer support to complete the worksheet.

Extension: Ask these learners to predict the shape of the magnetic field around a different type of magnet and then to test this using iron filings. They could draw the result on the back of their worksheet.

Wrapping up

- Talk through the answers to the worksheets together.
- **Answers: Worksheet 8.2a**

  1 a) Learners should have labelled their bar magnet with an 'N' and an 'S'.

  b)

Letter	What it represents
N	The north (magnetic) pole
S	The south (magnetic) pole

  2 a) repel

  b) attract

  3 a) Learners' diagrams to show field lines from N to S, with arrows pointing away from the N towards the S (as in Learner's Book 5, page 107).

  b) Look for answers which indicate that a magnetic field is the area of magnetic force which acts around a magnet.

- **Answers: Worksheet 8.2b**
  - Answers as for **Worksheet 8.2a**, apart from the level of detail expected for Question 3b:
  - **3 b)** Look for answers which include details such as the following: the magnetic field is an area of magnetic force around a magnet; field lines are invisible, but we can see them if we use iron filings; the magnetic field pattern shows the direction of the force from N to S poles of the magnet.

- **Extension activity:** Invite these learners to show their magnetic field diagrams for other magnets they chose.

- Remind learners that like poles repel (N–N or S–S) and opposite poles attract (N–S or S–N).

- The force you feel when bringing two magnets together is the strength of the magnetic field, whether the magnets attract or repel each other.

- Magnets produce force fields around them which are called magnetic fields.

- Magnetic fields are invisible but we can observe them using iron filings.

- Scientists use diagrams to show magnetic fields. The arrows always go from N to S poles.

Assessment for learning

Ask the learners:
- *What are the ends of a bar magnet called?*
- *What is the opposite of attraction?*
- *What is a magnetic field?*
- *Describe the direction of the arrows in a magnetic field diagram.*

8.3 Exploring magnets

Note: This material could be covered in two lessons, depending on the time available: Tests 1–3 in the first lesson and Tests 4–6 in the second lesson.

Resources

PowerPoint 8.3; Worksheets 8.3a and 8.3b (Boost); paper; markers; sticky tack; magnets; rulers with no gap between the end of the ruler and the zero; steel paper clips; magnetic surfaces, such as whiteboard or window frame; force meters; objects of different weights made of magnetic materials

Starter activity

- With talk partners or as a think–pair–share activity, ask learners to produce a mind map of everything they can remember about magnets so far.
- Display these as a gallery walk activity so learners can share their ideas. (Display the posters around the room and allow time for learners to visit those created by others to see what they have in common and the different facts others may have remembered. This serves as good assessment of prior knowledge.)

Main activities

- Display **PowerPoint 8.3**, which shows a copy of **Worksheet 8.3a**.
- Ask the learners to work in pairs or small groups.
- Give each pair a magnet and **Worksheet 8.3a** to complete as they do each test.
- The six activities on the worksheet can either be set up as a series of different workstations or, if there are sufficient resources for everyone, they can be left in a central area so learners can collect the resources as they need them.
- Work through the activities before allowing learners to begin.
  - **Test 1:** Place a paper clip on the table and stand a ruler on end beside it with the zero end on the table. (Make sure the end of the ruler starts at 0.) Slowly move the magnet down the side of the ruler towards the paper clip. The paper clip will be attracted to the magnet and will 'jump' off the table. Measure the height the clip reaches on the ruler when this happens.

- **Test 2:** Place a paper clip on the table and place a ruler (lying down) next to it with the zero end of the ruler next to the paper clip. Slowly move the magnet along the table beside the ruler towards the paper clip. The paper clip will be attracted to the magnet and will slide along the table. Measure the distance between the magnet and the starting point of the paper clip.
- **Test 3:** Find a vertical magnetic surface (such as a whiteboard or metal cupboard). Use the magnet to hold pieces of paper on the surface. Count the maximum number of pieces of paper the magnet can hold before it falls off.
- **Test 4:** Attach one paper clip to the magnet so that it hangs down. Add other paper clips one by one, but do **not** join them in a chain. Count how many paper clips can be held by the magnet in this way.
- **Test 5:** Find magnetic objects in the classroom that have different weights. Try using your magnet to pick each one up. *What is the heaviest object it can pick up?*
- **Test 6:** The metal hook on a force meter will be attracted to the magnet. *When you pull them apart, what force is required?*

Digging deeper

Support: Help these learners to take the force meter readings in Test 6.

Extension: Ask these learners to make groups of four to compare their results using **Worksheet 8.3b**.

Wrapping up

- Ask one learner to give their result for Test 1.
- Ask whether anyone had the same result.
- Repeat this for all the different tests.
- Ask the learners to think about why they have different answers.
- Make sure learners recognise that different magnets can have different strengths.

Assessment for learning

Ask the learners:
- *What is the same about all magnets?*
- *What can be different between magnets?*
- *Give an example of how the strength of a magnet can affect what it does.*

8.4 Testing the strength of magnets

Note: This material could be covered in two lessons, depending on the time available: the first lesson to plan and the second lesson to carry out the investigation.

Resources

PowerPoint 8.4; Worksheets 8.4a, 8.4b and 8.4c (Boost); internet access or reference books on magnetism

Starter activity

- Remind learners of the different tests they completed in the previous lesson.
  - Test 1: Making a paper clip 'jump'
  - Test 2: Making a paper clip slide
  - Test 3: Holding pieces of paper
  - Test 4: Number of paper clips held by the magnet
  - Test 5: Picking up different objects
  - Test 6: Separating the magnet from the hook on a force meter
- With talk partners, ask them to think about **why** each magnet gave different results in each test. (The magnets were different strengths.)
- Give all learners **Worksheet 8.4a**. Ask them to use the information to work out which is the strongest magnet and to rank the others from strongest to weakest.
- In talk partner pairs, give out **Worksheet 8.4b** for them to discuss the ideas on the worksheet.
- Explain how they will work in groups to think about the activities they carried out in the previous lesson. They will be expected to discuss how these ideas could be used to investigate the strength of different magnets.

Main activities

- Use **PowerPoint 8.4** to show the learners the table on **Worksheet 8.4a**.
- Share with the class how each of the six tests from the previous lesson could be used to investigate the strength of a magnet. Some tests will be quicker, some might be easier and some could give better results.
- Put learners into small groups and give one copy of **Worksheet 8.4c** to each group. Ask learners to

think about the good and bad points of each test and to record their ideas on this worksheet.

- Ask the learners to work in the same groups to decide on the best method to use for the investigation, bearing in mind the good and bad points they have just considered.
- Explain that they will need to keep their test fair. The only variable that should change is the magnet they are testing. They need to think about how they will keep their test fair, for example, by using the same-sized paper clips or the same thickness of paper. (This could be carried out in the next lesson, once they are secure in their planning.)

Digging deeper

Support: Remove some of the methods on **Worksheet 8.4c** for these learners to consider if working in a similar-ability group.

Extension: Ask these learners to research for homework where strong magnets are used in everyday life. (Look for ideas about modern trains, strong electromagnets being used in scrapyards, etc.)

Wrapping up

- Ask one learner from each group to explain which method they would choose to carry out the investigation, giving reasons why.
- Ask: *Which investigation do you think will be the quickest? Do you think any will take too long?*
- Ask: *Which investigation do you think will give the most accurate results? Do you think any will give insufficient evidence?*
- **Answers: Worksheet 8.4a**
  1 Magnet D
  2 Magnet D, Magnet A, Magnet B, Magnet C
- **Answers: Worksheet 8.4b**
  3 Sometimes the smaller magnet is stronger.

Assessment for learning

Ask the learners:
- *Did you identify good and/or bad points for each of the tests 1–6?*
- *Which method would you use?*
- *Why would you use that method?*

8 Unit assessment

Questions to ask

- *Name three different types of magnet.*
- *Name the opposite ends of a bar magnet.*
- *What do like poles do?*
- *Explain what happens when magnets repel each other.*

- *How can you show a magnetic field?*
- *Give one method for testing the strength of a magnet.*

Summative assessment activities

Observe the learners while they complete these activities. You will be able to quickly identify those who appear to be confident and those who might need additional support.

Magnets and magnetic materials

This activity provides an opportunity for learners to sort materials into magnetic and non-magnetic groups, and to consider the reasons why certain types of materials are magnetic.

You will need:
A collection of different objects, magnets, two plastic hoops for sorting

What to do
- Before learners carry out this activity, arrange the sorting hoops side by side.
- Ask learners to test the objects and materials available with a magnet and then sort them into two groups.
- When they have finished, ask them why they have grouped the objects and materials in this way. Record their reasons.

- Ask them to give you the scientific vocabulary that categorises each group.
- Then ask them to say a) which materials are attracted to the magnet (don't use the term 'magnetic') and b) why.

Magnetic strength
This activity enables learners to share their reasoning about magnetic strength. It will involve them in thinking and working scientifically.

You will need:
A set of different types of magnet, steel paper clips

What to do
- Ask the learners to use the magnets and paper clips to compare the strengths of the magnets.
- Observe their actions and how they choose to record any results.
- Ask: *Which magnet is the strongest? How do you know?* Repeat for the weakest magnet.

Written assessment
Distribute **Worksheet 8.5**. The learners should work independently or with their usual in-class support.

Unit 9 Planet Earth

Prior learning

Learners should be able to recall how Earth is the source of many everyday materials such as oil, natural gas and metals. They should also know the basic structure of Earth: core, mantle and crust.

Science in context

Lesson 9.10 provides an opportunity for some learners to research industrial uses of evaporation, for example, in the production of rock salt.

9.1 Earth's atmosphere

Resources

PowerPoint 9.1; Worksheet 9.1 (Boost); mirrors or ceramic tiles; kettle full of water; heat source to heat the water in the kettle; whiteboard or flipchart and markers; internet access; pizza/circle of paper, burger/picture of a burger, jug, water, stone and tea leaves (all optional)

Starter activity

- With talk partners, ask learners to discuss: *What is in Earth's atmosphere?*
- Share their responses and list learners' ideas and thoughts on the whiteboard or flipchart.
- Tell them they will now watch a video to see how many of their ideas were correct.
- Use **PowerPoint 9.1** to show a video of Earth's atmosphere. Note: the important facts learners need to know are simply that Earth is surrounded by a layer of air called the atmosphere and that air is a mixture of gases, including nitrogen (approximately 77 % according to this video), oxygen (21 %) and a few other gases including carbon dioxide and argon (2 % total). Learners do **not** need to remember the different layers of the atmosphere at Stage 5.

Main activities

- Alternatively, or as well as watching the video, use the video for teacher preparation and model the activities shown to demonstrate:
  - the percentage composition of gases in the atmosphere (by cutting up a pizza or circle of paper)
  - the different layers in the atmosphere (by using the model of a burger)
  - the pressure in the different layers of the atmosphere using a jug of water, a stone and tea leaves.
- Give all learners **Worksheet 9.1**.
- Play the video again and ask them to complete the worksheet as they watch the video.

Misconceptions

Some learners might think air is empty. Ask learners to breathe out onto a cold surface, such as a mirror or ceramic tile. (Note that how successful the outcome of this is may depend on how warm your environment is.) Explain to learners that their breath contains water vapour (this can be seen easily when breathing out in cold weather conditions). Water vapour is a gas, which cools down on the cold surface and turns into water droplets; in other words, it condenses. (There is more about this in later lessons. Condensation was also covered in Lesson 5.5 in Unit 5 of this stage.)

To further demonstrate this, boil a kettle until steam appears. The steam then seems to disappear; at this point the visible water droplets have become water vapour, which is water in its gaseous state.

Some learners might think air is a single gas, rather than a mixture of gases. The video confirms the approximate percentage composition of air.

Digging deeper

Support: Give extra time to these learners and allow them to watch the video as many times as they need to complete **Worksheet 9.1**.

Extension: Ask these learners to do more research into the layers in the atmosphere, or just one of them.

Wrapping up

- Talk through the answers to **Worksheet 9.1** together.
- **Answers:**

  1 a) nitrogen, oxygen and carbon dioxide
  b) 77 %, 21 % and 2 %

2 Correct answers will describe Earth's atmosphere as a layer of air (which is a mixture of different gases). This air comprises mainly nitrogen and oxygen with a small amount of carbon dioxide and some other gases, including argon.

Assessment for learning

Ask the learners:
- *What is Earth's atmosphere?*
- *What are some of the main gases in Earth's atmosphere?*
- *What percentage of the atmosphere do they make up?*

9.2 Global warming (the greenhouse effect)

Resources

PowerPoint 9.2; Worksheet 9.2 (Boost); internet access; globe

Starter activity

- Ask the learners to discuss in pairs: *What is global warming? What are greenhouse gases?* This will give you an indication about how much or how little the learners already know.
- Listen to their responses and explain that, in this lesson, they will find out more about these things.

Main activities

- Display **PowerPoint 9.2**, slide 1, which shows an image of global warming and gives the definition of it as 'the rise in temperature of Earth's atmosphere'. The PowerPoint notes also include the following text: Did you know, it is predicted that if a baby born in 2022 lives to be 80 years old, world temperatures will be more than 6 degrees higher than world temperatures recorded in 2022?
- Display **PowerPoint 9.2**, slide 2, which shows an image representing Earth and greenhouse gases. There are notes at the bottom of the PowerPoint, as follows: Greenhouse gases are water vapour, carbon dioxide, methane, nitrous oxide, ozone, chlorofluorocarbons (CFCs). They are all natural gases, but extra greenhouses gases can be made by humans from pollution.
- Give out **Worksheet 9.2** to all learners and use **PowerPoint 9.2**, slide 3, to explain the diagram of Earth and its atmosphere (see PowerPoint notes). Explain how the Sun's rays penetrate Earth's atmosphere and maintain Earth's temperature, which ensures the survival of animals and plants. Explain (or ask the learners) about things that contribute to Earth's temperature rising (carbon dioxide (CO_2) being exhaled, Earth's growing population so there is more CO_2 produced from people as well as from factories, vehicles and so on).

- Describe the CO_2 as forming a blanket which traps heat and means that, over time (within the next century), scientists are predicting temperature rises of more than 6 °C.
- As a class, discuss what this will mean for us on Earth (use the globe as a reference):
  - Glaciers and sea ice at the poles will melt. This means sea levels will rise, which will cause flooding in low-lying areas.
  - Lakes and rivers will dry up and, in some areas, this could create drought conditions. Ask: *How might this affect crop growing in these areas?*
  - Winds could get stronger or travel from different directions, so there will be more tornadoes and hurricanes.
  - There will be less water available to us on Earth. Think about all the things we need water for on a daily basis.
  - Some animals and plants could become extinct due to the changes in their environment.
- Ask learners to complete **Worksheet 9.2** either now or for homework.

Digging deeper

Support: Work with these learners in a small group to make sure they understand the diagram.

Extension: Ask these learners to find out about some sources of alternative (cleaner) energy being trialled around the world; for example, wind, wave, solar or hydroelectric power (HEP).

Wrapping up

- Talk through the answers to **Worksheet 9.2** together.
- **Answers: 1** Earth, **2** Sun, **3** atmosphere, **4** greenhouse gases, **5** pollution, **6** fossil fuels, **7** deforestation

Assessment for learning

Ask the learners:
- *What is global warming?*
- *Name some greenhouse gases.*
- *What might happen on Earth as a consequence of global warming?*
- *What are scientists suggesting as good alternatives to those things that contribute to global warming?*

9.3 The ozone layer

Resources

PowerPoint 9.3; Worksheet 9.3 (Boost); globe; aerosol spray; sticky labels with the letter O on them; pair of sunglasses suitable for your class age group; masks (the type that cover the eyes with eye slits in them and have elastic to hold them on); large open space outside or indoors

Starter activity

- Use the globe to remind the learners that Earth is surrounded by its atmosphere and a layer of greenhouse gases.
- Re-introduce the word 'ozone' (first used as an example of a greenhouse gas in the previous lesson) and describe it as the ozone layer, which protects Earth from harmful UV (ultraviolet) rays from the Sun.
- Display **PowerPoint 9.3**, slide 1, which shows an image of an aerosol can being sprayed. Ask the learners how the aerosol works, then explain that the gas inside the aerosol pushes out the liquid as a fine spray.

Main activities

- Display **PowerPoint 9.3**, slide 2, which shows an image of the ozone layer.
- Explain how scientists discovered that holes were being formed in the ozone layer by the over-use of aerosols and some other chemicals called CFCs (also mentioned in the previous lesson). CFCs were used in old refrigerators and freezers to keep them cool. They are no longer used.
- Take the class outside or into a large, indoor space such as the gymnasium. Use the following activity to help learners understand how CFCs damaged the ozone layer.
  - Choose some pairs of learners to be oxygen molecules. Give them each a sticker with the letter O on it.
  - Choose another learner to be the Sun and give them the sunglasses to wear.
  - Choose more learners to be CFCs. These learners should wear the masks.
  - Each pair wearing the 'O' stickers represents an oxygen molecule. The Sun learner must

touch an oxygen pair on the shoulder, which makes them split apart and go off to find another oxygen molecule.
- When they join up as a three, they become an ozone molecule. This does not last long, as the oxygen atoms prefer to be in pairs, so the ozone molecule splits again. This happens all the time in the ozone layer.
- Then, along come the nasty CFCs! They 'steal' oxygen atoms and make poisonous gases. (Invite the learners representing the CFCs to run around among the oxygen molecules.) This means that there is less ozone formed and it is not able to protect Earth effectively from the harmful UV rays from the Sun.
- Give out **Worksheet 9.3** to all learners and ask them to draw a cartoon strip of this process.

Digging deeper

Support: Work with these learners in a small group or form mixed-ability groups.
Extension: Ask these learners to act as narrators for other groups.

Wrapping up

- Talk about how the United Nations is committed to Sustainable Development: 2020 and Beyond. The year 2020 marked the start of the Decade of Action to deliver the Sustainable Development Goals by 2030. Use internet research to find out more about what is proposed and how the United Nations intends to achieve this.
- Create a display space for learners to show and share their cartoons.

Assessment for learning

Ask the learners:
- *Where is the ozone layer?*
- *Why are CFCs harmful?*
- *What is ozone made from?*
- *Name one way that we can we reduce damage in the ozone layer.*

9.4 How humans can affect the environment

Resources

PowerPoint 9.4; Worksheet 9.4 (Boost); whiteboard or flipchart and markers

Starter activity

- Use **PowerPoint 9.4** to ask the learners what is meant by the term 'environment'. Discuss their answers and agree a joint definition. Write and display this prominently.

- A simple definition of environment is 'the local area, weather and landscape where something lives'. This definition is also in the PowerPoint slide notes and the vocabulary list. Share this with the class.

- Explain how your school environment is the buildings and grounds; in other words, the whole school site.

- As a class, discuss ways in which we should care for the school environment. Listen to the learners' suggestions. Lead the discussion to ensure it covers points such as keeping it clean, making sure water is safe to drink and looking after animals and plants in the school grounds.

- Working in pairs, ask learners to discuss ways in which human activities can destroy environments.

- Listen to the learners' responses and ensure they mention dropping litter and wasting water, electricity and paper.

- Perhaps also discuss more environmentally friendly ways of travelling to school; for example, walking, cycling or catching the school bus rather than arriving by car.

Main activities

- Explain that some of the things humans do can have a positive impact and so are good for the environment. Other things that humans do can have a negative impact, which means that these things are not good for the environment.

- Also explain how, as part of the natural world along with other animals and plants, we are dependent on each other.

- As a class, talk about how we need clean air and water, and good growing conditions for plants, which animals eat. Ultimately, if we are meat-eaters, these animals may form part of our diet.

- Give out **Worksheet 9.4** to all learners to record some of the negative and positive impacts that human activity can have on the environment.

Digging deeper

Support: Discuss answers as a small group with these learners before they complete **Worksheet 9.4**.

Extension: Ask these learners to identify something that is happening locally that is having either a positive or negative effect on the local environment. (For instance, litter picking on a beach or in a park; local areas seeded with wildflowers and designated as 'bee-friendly' zones.)

Wrapping up

- Discuss the learners' responses to **Worksheet 9.4**.

- Correct answers will include such things as:
  - **Positive effects:** keeping the environment litter free; making water supplies clean and safe; looking after animals and plants to help them thrive; walking or cycling to school
  - **Negative effects:** dropping litter; wasting water, electricity and paper; using cars and other petrol or diesel vehicles.

- Make sure learners understand the definition of what the environment is. Refer back to the PowerPoint slide again, if necessary.

Assessment for learning

Ask the learners:

- *What does 'environment' mean?*
- *Name one positive effect humans can have on the environment.*
- *Describe a negative effect that humans can have on the environment.*
- *Why is it important for us to take good care of animals and plants?*
- *What things that are good or bad for the environment are happening locally?*

9.5 Acid rain

Resources

PowerPoint 9.5; Worksheets 9.5a and 9.5b (Boost); 50 ml clean drinking water in a beaker; pre-prepared red cabbage indicator; 50 ml of lemon juice in a beaker; 50 ml of white vinegar in a beaker; large screw-top glass jar; distilled water; safety matches; sticks of chalk to crush

Starter activity

- Use **PowerPoint 9.5**, slides 1–3, to show images of a volcano, a power station burning a fossil fuel, and vehicle exhaust fumes. Show the learners the slides one by one and, as a class, discuss what types of pollution these all produce. (Volcanoes produce nasty-smelling gases; fossil fuels produce soot and smoke, and give off gases into the air; vehicle exhaust emissions also release gases into the air.)
- Show the sample of water.

Main activities

- Explain that the smoke and/or fumes produced by volcanoes, power stations and vehicles dissolve in rain as it falls and make acid rain.
- Rain is also made acidic by carbon dioxide (the same gas that we all breathe out). Acid rain can affect trees as it falls, sometimes even causing them to die.
- Demonstrate the acidity of acid rain using red cabbage indicator. (This can be made by boiling red cabbage in a small amount of water, to make the indicator concentrated. Let it cool and store it. Note that it does not keep well. The indicator turns red in the presence of an acid, is purple when neutral and in alkaline solutions it turns blue or green.)
- Give out **Worksheet 9.5a** for the learners to complete as you do the demonstration.
- Mix a few drops of red cabbage indicator with the drinking water and note the colour.
- Mix a few drops of the indicator with the white vinegar and then the lemon juice. Note the colour changes.
- Now simulate acid rain: quarter-fill the glass jar with distilled water. Add a few drops of red cabbage indicator. Then light several safety matches in the glass jar above the water. When they finish burning, blow them out and quickly put the lid on the jar. Shake it and observe the colour change in the indicator in the jar.
- Then add some crushed chalk to the water, shake it again and observe what happens (chalk dissolves, some fizzing may be observed and more colour change). This demonstrates the effect of acid rain on soft rock.

Misconceptions

Some learners might think the term 'pollution' also applies to natural phenomena such as volcanoes and forest fires which harm the environment. Explain that pollutants only exist because they are created as a result of human activity. For this reason, we do not refer to natural emissions from the Earth as pollution.

Digging deeper

Support: Work closely with these learners in completing **Worksheet 9.5a**.

Extension: Give these learners **Worksheet 9.5b**. Alternatively, use this as another class lesson on the effects of acid rain.

Wrapping up

- Discuss the learners' observations and the colour changes observed (refer to the notes above).
- As a class, talk about ways in which scientists today are suggesting we can reduce the amount of air pollution, which creates acid rain. Examples could include using cleaner or renewable fuels or using fewer vehicles and more public transport.
- **Answers: Worksheet 9.5a**

1

Liquid	Colour	Colour with red cabbage indicator
red cabbage indicator	dark blue	
drinking water	clear/ transparent	purple
lemon juice	pale yellow	red

Liquid	Colour	Colour with red cabbage indicator
white vinegar	clear/ transparent	red
acid rain (in jar)	cloudy, white liquid	red

2 The chalk dissolves, some fizzing may be observed and colour change to blue/green occurs.

3 Red

4 a) White vinegar is a strong acid.

   b) Acid rain is a weaker acid.

- **Answers: Worksheet 9.5b**

   1 open-ended

   2 Correct answers will include ideas about how the acid rain erodes (eats into) the soft rock and it starts to disintegrate over time.

Assessment for learning

Ask the learners:

- *How does acid rain form?*
- *What kinds of pollution help create acid rain?*
- *Which gas contributes to acid rain being formed?*
- *What can acid rain do to buildings?*

9.6 Collecting evidence of pollution in the air

Note: This material could be split into two lessons, depending on the time available.

Resources

PowerPoint 9.6; Worksheets 9.6a and 9.6b (Boost); internet access or reference books; whiteboard or flipchart and markers; filter funnels and filter papers; beakers; water; plan of the school grounds; white ceramic tiles (or card, double-sided sticky tape and scissors); evergreen leaves

Starter activity

- Organise the learners into pairs and then ask them to name as many examples of sources of air pollution as they can in two minutes.
- Collect their responses on the flipchart/ whiteboard without commenting on them.
- Use **PowerPoint 9.6** to show pictures of sources of air pollution from around the world. Discuss their responses. Ask: *Did you identify all the sources on the slide? Did you identify any others?* If they did, add these to the class list.
- As a class, discuss and compare living in a city to living in the countryside: *Would there be any difference in the amount of pollution? Can you name any big cities around the world that are badly polluted?*

Main activities

- Explain how pollution leaves dry, sooty materials in the air. In this lesson, learners will find out whether there is any evidence of air pollution near to the school.
- Give out **Worksheets 9.6a** and **9.6b** to all learners. Look at these photocopiable pages with the learners, making sure they know what to do.
- Discuss what evergreen leaves are: these are leaves that remain on the tree, bush or plant all year round.
- Define and/or mark out areas in the school grounds where learners are allowed to look for evergreen leaves, or send different pairs or small groups to specific areas of the school grounds. (Have some collected evergreen leaves ready in case the learners are unable to find any of their own. If these are not available, use photos of leaves from the internet.)
- Demonstrate (or ask the learners if they can remember) how to fold a filter paper for use with a filter funnel.
- Direct (or allow the learners to choose) places to leave the white tiles or sticky-taped cards. (You could mark these places on a plan of the school.)
- Organise the learners into pairs or small groups to carry out these activities.

Misconceptions

Explain that pollutants only exist because they are created by human activity, not as a result of natural catastrophes such as volcanoes and earthquakes.

Digging deeper

Support: Either allow these learners to work in mixed-ability groups or work with them in a small group.

Extension: Ask these learners to identify any evergreen leaves found, using the internet to search or any reference books available.

Wrapping up

- Bring the class back together and discuss learners' findings.
- **Answers: Worksheet 9.6a**
  - The leaves drawn will differ according to your location in the world.
  - **Results:** Depending on where the leaf was picked, the filtered water will contain varying amounts of particles, dust and/or dirt – some visible and some not visible particles – which could be due to pollutants.
- **Answers: Worksheet 9.6b:** open-ended responses

Assessment for learning

Ask the learners:
- *What is an evergreen leaf?*
- *What was left behind when you filtered the water?*
- *What did you see on the white tile/ sticky tape?*
- *Where did you find evidence of most pollution?*
- *What might be the biggest causes of air pollution close to the school?*

9.7 Environmental damage

Resources

PowerPoint 9.7; Worksheets 9.7a and 9.7b (Boost); candle in tray of sand; white tile or piece of safety glass; tongs; internet access or reference books

Starter activity

- Look back at the results from the previous lesson. Ask the learners: *What was the main indicator of environmental pollution?*
- Working in pairs, ask learners to talk about where this soot came from.

Main activities

- Demonstrate holding a white tile or piece of safety glass over a burning candle (using tongs).
- Make sure that the candle is securely fixed in a tray of sand and that the learners are seated a safe distance away as you do the demonstration.
- Show the surface of the tile or glass blackened with soot.
- Ask the learners: *What else does a candle produce when it burns?* Explain that soot and gases are the waste products of burning.
- Use **PowerPoint 9.7** to show pictures of emissions from vehicles in a busy city and emissions from an aeroplane.
- Discuss whether the learners know any ways in which such sources of pollution are dangerous to humans over time. (Exhaust fumes contain poisonous gases, which can cause allergies and intolerances in some people. Breathing in badly polluted air has been known to cause brain damage over time, particularly in children, who have smaller lungs. Treat this issue carefully as some of the learners may have family members with respiratory diseases. Also, learners this age are very sensitive to thoughts of things that might kill them!)

- Explain how the use of unleaded fuels for vehicles is being increased in many countries, which will reduce the level of poisonous gases in the air over time. In the 2020s, increasing numbers of people are choosing to buy electric cars, which do not produce exhaust fumes.

- Explain that, in Ulaanbaatar, the capital city of Mongolia, new bus lanes have been introduced. Also, car drivers can only drive in the city on certain days. Discuss the difference this might make. (Less traffic congestion, more people using public transport, less pollution from vehicles, etc.)

- Give out **Worksheet 9.7a** to learners who need support. Give out **Worksheet 9.7b** to all other learners for them to complete.

Digging deeper

Support: Give these learners **Worksheet 9.7a**, a wordsearch about pollution.

Extension: Ask these learners to write a leaflet encouraging the use of electric cars, or to research an electric car they might like to own and drive as an adult.

Wrapping up

- Talk through the answers to the worksheets.
- **Answers: Worksheet 9.7a**

1

s	o	b	r	k	y	m	p
l	i	r	u	g	r	t	o
k	p	e	t	r	o	l	y
e	r	a	p	t	n	o	g
c	u	t	g	l	i	b	a
i	v	h	r	e	s	p	s
i	s	e	m	u	f	l	e
n	e	p	y	t	o	o	s

2 Pollution is bad for humans because it can cause breathing difficulties and allergies.

- **Answers: Worksheet 9.7b**

⇨ (accept in any order) **a)** vehicle emissions, **b)** factory emissions, **c)** aeroplane emissions

2 Accept answers which include ideas about encouraging more use of public transport, cycling or walking; less use of fossil fuels/use of cleaner (green) energy, etc.

3 open-ended responses

- Hold a class discussion, asking: *What might you suggest to reduce air pollution if you lived in Ulaanbaatar?* (or indeed if they actually do)

Assessment for learning

Ask the learners:
- *What are the waste products of burning?*
- *Why is pollution a concern in big cities?*
- *How are some governments attempting to reduce levels of air pollution?*
- *How can pollution affect our health?*

9.8 Deforestation

Resources

PowerPoint 9.8; Worksheet 9.8 (Boost); internet access or reference books

Starter activity

- Use **PowerPoint 9.8**, which has a partial map of South America and shows the size of the Amazon rainforest.

- Working in pairs, ask learners to decide on a definition of 'deforestation'. (The definition should include the idea of cutting down, clearing and removing forests.)

- Ask the learners: *What are some possible causes of deforestation?* (They include farming, cattle ranching, logging, mining and extraction of oil or gas.)

Main activities

- Discuss with the learners what happens when rainforest is cleared: fertile soil that is good for farming gets washed away quickly. Profits from large-scale farming and sales of the produce grown go back to big global companies and do not benefit the locals who live and work in or near the rainforest. Agriculture is now thought to be responsible for more than a quarter of the Amazon rainforest clearance, although mining and transport needs also cause deforestation.

- Explain how sometimes forests are cleared for new roads to be built. This separates areas within the rainforest and could mean that some species of animals (monkeys, for example) might find it more difficult to get their food. If they do not eat as much food, they will not produce as much waste, which can contain seeds from plants they have eaten, so fewer new plants will grow.

- When trees are cut down, animals and plants have to adapt to the different conditions – less shade, loss of habitat, etc. Some species might even become extinct as a result. Large rainforest trees take many years to grow.

- Give out **Worksheet 9.8** for all learners to complete about the effects of deforestation.

Digging deeper

Support: Work in a small group with these learners, discussing their responses as they complete **Worksheet 9.8**.

Extension: Ask these learners to research an animal on the verge of extinction or an animal that has already become extinct. Give them internet access and/or reference books, or set this activity for homework. Give them free choice in how to present their research findings.

Wrapping up

- Discuss as a class: *What are the consequences of deforestation?*

- **Answers to Worksheet 9.8:**

  1 Correct answers will include some detail about:
   a) **Farming:** fertile soil, good for growing plants, can get washed away. Local farmers do not benefit from profits made.
   b) **Road building:** new roads separate different areas in the rainforest. This might make it difficult for some animals to get enough food. Often seeds from plants eaten by animals are transferred in their waste; eating less food means fewer plants will grow.
   c) **Mining:** spoils good soil or ground; trees cut down means loss of habitats.

  2 'Extinct' means a group of living things that have died out altogether (such as dodos).

  3 Open-ended responses which could include dodo, great auk, woolly mammoth, West African black rhinoceros, etc.

Assessment for learning

Ask the learners:
- *What is the name of the large rainforest in South America?*
- *What is deforestation?*
- *Why do forests sometimes need to be cut down?*
- *Why is this a bad thing?*

9.9 What can we do?

Resources

PowerPoint 9.9; Worksheets 9.9a and 9.9b (Boost); art materials or an ICT publishing package to make posters; felt-tip pens or colouring pencils

Starter activity

- Working in pairs, ask learners to discuss ways in which they are aware of reducing, reusing and recycling things at home.
- Listen to their answers and explain how, in this lesson, they will be thinking about ways to reduce, reuse and recycle things.

Main activities

- Talk about each of these areas – reducing, reusing and recycling – in turn.
- Ask learners: *What can people do to reduce the use of things which damage the environment?* (If they struggle, suggest one of the following: buy a smaller car, try an electric car or a hybrid, take public transport, car-share, walk or cycle.)
- This discussion may also lead to learners talking about reducing the use of chemicals or pesticides by farmers and/or using less plastic and paper in packaging.
- Ask the learners: *What kinds of things can we easily reuse?*
- Some of them may know about internet sites where things can be passed on or sold instead of being thrown away.
- Suggest organising a 'swap shop' for toys or books (with permission from home and the school management) to encourage other learners to begin to think about reusing things.
- Use **PowerPoint 9.9**, which shows the recycling logo. Ask learners if they recognise it. Explain how this logo means that the object it appears on can be recycled. As a class, talk about any of the recycling facilities (if any) available in school or locally.
- The main things to be recycled are usually plastic, glass, metals, paper and clothes. Ask: *How can we encourage better recycling at home and school?*
- Give out **Worksheets 9.9a** and **9.9b** for learners to record their own ideas about reducing, reusing and recycling.

Digging deeper

Support: Work with these learners in a small group and ask them to give only one example of something we can reduce the use of, reuse and recycle.

Extension: Ask these learners to produce a poster to encourage people to be more environmentally friendly in school. Display these posters prominently around the school site.

Wrapping up

- Discuss the main messages again: we need to look after the things we have and be careful, not wasteful.
- Repeat: remember to reduce, reuse and recycle!
- **Answers: Worksheet 9.9a**

1
Item	Alternative	Reason
fossil fuels	greener fuels or electricity	reduces pollution
paper	electronic versions	saves trees
plastics	natural materials	prevents seas being polluted and animals being harmed

This is not an exhaustive list.

2 See **Worksheet 9.9b**.

3

4 Correct answers will include examples such as paper, clothes, cars, glass, aluminium cans, some plastics.

- **Answers: Worksheet 9.9b**
  - Invitations should be bright and eye-catching.

Assessment for learning

Ask the learners:
- *What are the three Rs of being environmentally aware?*
- *Tell me something that we should reduce our use of, how and why.*
- *What could we reuse more?*
- *What things do we recycle?*

9.10 The water cycle

Resources

PowerPoint 9.10; Worksheet 9.10 (Boost); beakers or jars; water; measuring cylinders; internet access; heat source; tile or mirror; poster paper; collage or art materials; scissors; glue; pre-printed vocabulary labels

Starter activity

- Set up a container of water in a warm place.
- Measure the volume of water at the beginning of the day/lesson and at regular intervals throughout the day, during the lesson or over the course of several lessons. Record the results.
- Discuss what has happened when it is noticeable that some of the water has evaporated.
- Ask the learners: *How can we get back the lost water?*
- Ask them to predict how quickly all the water might evaporate.

Main activities

- Demonstrate rapid evaporation by boiling water. Measure the starting volume of water used.
- Show the learners that water vapour can be turned back into water droplets by being cooled down. Hold a mirror or tile in the water vapour and observe the droplets forming.
- Reintroduce the term 'condensation' and describe what it is. (It was covered in Lesson 5.5 of this stage.) Measure the volume of condensed water collected. Discuss findings.
- Ask the learners to give any examples from everyday life when they might have seen evidence of evaporation or condensation; for example, puddles drying up, clothes drying, condensation in the bathroom on tiles or windows.
- Use **PowerPoint 9.10**, slide 1, to show a video of the water cycle.
- Introduce the relevant scientific vocabulary associated with the water cycle: evaporation, condensation and precipitation.
- Talk through the water cycle using these terms and discuss what happens at each stage.
- Use **PowerPoint 9.10**, slide 2, to show a diagram of the water cycle.

- Give out **Worksheet 9.10** for all learners, or just to learners who need support, to complete. Ask learners who have not been given the worksheet to draw and label their own diagram of the water cycle using these words: condensation, evaporation and precipitation.

Misconceptions

Some learners might think rain (precipitation) is made in the air, rather than being part of the water cycle. Make sure this is made clear when you explain the water cycle using the video and the diagram in **PowerPoint 9.10**.

Digging deeper

Support: Make a group collage or poster of the water cycle with these learners. Ask them to label the stages using pre-printed labels. Display and show the completed work to the rest of the class.

Extension: Ask these learners to research useful examples of evaporation around the world, such as salt production by evaporation of salt pools.

Wrapping up

- Invite some learners to share their completed work with the rest of the class.
- Praise correct use of scientific vocabulary.
- Make sure they know the importance of being able to spell these words correctly.
- Talk about the inverse relationship between evaporation and condensation, in that condensation is the reverse of evaporation.
- **Answers: Worksheet 9.10:** precipitation (left label); condensation (top right); evaporation (bottom right).

Assessment for learning

Ask the learners:
- *What is evaporation?*
- *How does condensation form?*
- *What is the scientific name for rain?*
- *How are the processes of evaporation and condensation related?*

9 Unit assessment

Questions to ask

- *Tell me one way in which we can look after our local environment.*
- *Describe a negative effect that human activity can have on the environment.*
- *What is the process called when people cut down forests?*

- *Name some materials that can be recycled.*
- *How can we reduce our use of fossil fuels?*
- *If we were to do one more thing in school to care for the environment, what thing do you think would make the most difference?*

Summative assessment activities

Observe the learners while they complete these activities. You will be able to quickly identify those who appear to be confident and those who might need additional support.

Recycling

This activity assesses the learners' understanding of recyclable materials.

You will need:

Rubbish bag or waste bin (make sure this is clean); selection of empty packets, tins, jars and boxes, typical of 'rubbish' from a bin at home (ensure it is all safe, clean and that there are no sharp edges); digital camera

What to do

- Ask the learners as individuals to sort through the rubbish and re-group it for recycling.
- Discuss with them their choices as they carry out the activity or when they have finished.
- Differentiate the activity by asking learners of different abilities to sort more or fewer items.
- Record the outcomes. Take a digital photograph for evidence, if required.

Making compost

This activity assesses the learners' understanding of using recyclable materials to create compost.

You will need:

Plastic or paper cups; compost; magnifying glass; plastic gloves; soil; twigs; leaves; newspaper; water

What to do

- Show the learners the compost. Ask them if they know what it is. If they do not, tell them and explain that this is nature's way of recycling! Allow them to look at it using a magnifying glass.
- Ask them to use the other things provided to make their own compost. Talk to them about each ingredient and why they have included it.
- List their ingredients and make notes about what the learners say about them.

Written assessment

Give learners time to complete **Worksheet 9.11**. The learners should work independently or with their usual in-class support.

Unit 10 Earth in space

Prior learning

Learners should be able to explain why the spinning of Earth on its axis leads to night and day, the apparent movement of the Sun, and changes in shadows.

Science in context

Lesson 10.4 provides an opportunity for learners to find out about space junk.

10.1 Earth, Sun and Moon

Resources

PowerPoint 10.1; Worksheets 10.1a and 10.1b (Boost); internet access; large, inflatable ball; sticky note or label; globe; computer design package (if available); art materials including drawing paper, pencils, pens or paints

Starter activity

- Give out **Worksheet 10.1a** to all learners. Ask them to draw an annotated diagram of the Earth, Sun and Moon. (This is revision and will indicate to you how much they have remembered from previous work.)
- Invite some of the learners – maybe one learner who needs support, an average-ability learner and then a learner who needs extension work – to share and describe what they have drawn.
- Keep them in this order, asking each one to give more information than the previous learner.
- Use **PowerPoint 10.1**, which shows a video of the movements of Earth and the Moon in space relative to the Sun. Talk about what they remembered and whether they have remembered correctly. Ask: *Did you get the positions correct? Did you show the different sizes correctly?*

Main activities

- Recall how the Sun **does not** move. Learners should remember that Earth orbits the Sun. Explain that the Sun is at the centre of our planetary system.
- Demonstrate this by asking one of the learners to hold the large, inflatable ball. If it helps, label this 'Sun'. Then, using the globe, 'orbit' the Sun – that is, physically walk around the 'Sun' – holding the globe, and explain that the time taken for this to happen is one year (365¼ days).
- Next, demonstrate Earth (globe) revolving on its axis. Show the learners the imaginary axis that goes from the north pole to the south pole.
- Explain and show that, at the same time as it is orbiting the Sun, Earth is rotating on its own axis (this is a difficult concept).
- Give all learners **Worksheet 10.1b** to complete.

Misconceptions

Some learners might think Earth stays still and the Sun orbits Earth. The video in the Starter activity shows that this is not what happens and, in fact, Earth orbits the Sun.

Digging deeper

Support: Pre-prepare a diagram of the relative positions of the Earth, Sun and Moon on **Worksheet 10.1a** so these learners can simply annotate the diagram.

Extension: Ask these learners to think of another way to model Earth's movements. They could use a computer design package (if available) or produce a poster.

Wrapping up

- **Answers: Worksheet 10.1a**
  1 Refer to **PowerPoint 10.1** for an image of the Earth, Sun and Moon and their relative sizes and positions to each other in space.
  2 **Sun:** stays still; **Earth:** rotates on its own axis and orbits the Sun; **Moon:** orbits Earth

● **Answers: Worksheet 10.1b**

1 Earth orbits the Sun (answer provided); The Sun stays still; Earth spins on its own axis; A year takes 365¼ days

2 Earth spins on its own axis and orbits the Sun.

3 a year or 365¼ days

10.2 Earth's elliptical orbit

Resources

PowerPoint 10.2; Worksheet 10.2 (Boost); collage, poster-making or art materials; large ball for the Sun; globe or another ball to represent Earth; internet access or reference books about year length

Starter activity

- Ask learners to discuss these questions in pairs: *What shape is Earth? What shape is the Sun?*

- Use **PowerPoint 10.2**, slide 1, which shows an image of Earth spinning. Use this diagram to explain the term 'axis' as the point about which Earth spins or rotates. The axis runs from the north pole to the south pole through the centre of Earth. Describe how one rotation on this axis takes one day or 24 hours. Also ask about or explain about the equator: an imaginary line drawn around the middle of Earth's surface, at equal distances from the two poles.

- Use **PowerPoint 10.2**, slide 2, which shows an image of the path of Earth's orbit around the Sun. Ask learners to describe the shape of the orbit. Some learners will identify it as circular but show how it is a 'squashed' circle. Introduce the word 'elliptical' to describe this.

Main activities

- Explain that Earth travels around the Sun in an anticlockwise direction. Model this using a ball for the Sun and a globe or another ball to represent Earth.

- Give all learners **Worksheet 10.2** to complete.

- In small groups, if time allows, ask learners to make a poster or model showing Earth's elliptical orbit.

Misconceptions

Some learners might still think that Earth stays still and the Sun orbits Earth. Keep reinforcing the idea that the Sun remains still while Earth and other planets orbit it.

Digging deeper

Support: Model Earth revolving around the Sun as many times as necessary to help these learners understand.

Extension: Ask these learners to research what a leap year is. When they have done this, check answers and explain/confirm that every four years, February has an extra day to accommodate the ¼ day out of the 365¼ days it takes Earth to orbit the Sun. We say that a year is 365 days and a leap year day every four years compensates for this.

Wrapping up

- Talk through the answers to **Worksheet 10.2**.

1

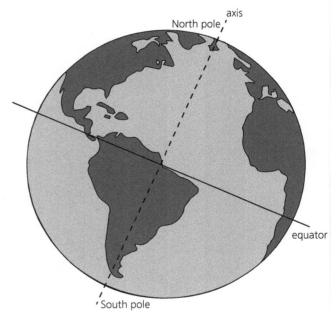

2 elliptical
3 anticlockwise

- **Extension activity:** refer to above notes about leap years.

Assessment for learning

Ask the learners:

- *What is Earth's axis?*
- *How many times does Earth rotate on its axis each day?*
- *What is the equator?*
- *What word best describes the shape of Earth's orbit of the Sun?*
- *How long does it take Earth to orbit the Sun?*

10.3 Seasons

Resources

PowerPoint 10.3; Worksheet 10.3 (Boost); protractor/angle measurer; globe; flashlight; internet access or reference books about seasons around the world

Starter activity

- Ask learners, in pairs, to discuss how many seasons they experience each year where they live. This will vary around the world; some will have four seasons, others just two. For example, in the tropical and sub-tropical regions, there are only two seasons. These are usually called the monsoon or wet season and the dry season.

- Also ask learners to discuss why it is hotter in summer and cooler in winter. Again, this varies around the world. This will be explained later in the lesson.

- Use **PowerPoint 10.3**, slide 1, which shows a diagram of seasons in the northern hemisphere. Note the tilt of Earth and the order in which seasons occur, remembering the anticlockwise travel of Earth around the Sun.

Main activities

- Use **PowerPoint 10.3**, slide 2, which shows a diagram of the angle of tilt of Earth (23.5°) and how it always points in the same direction. You will need a protractor/angle measurer (you might have used this in maths lessons). Talk about the northern and southern hemispheres, and which hemisphere you live in.

- Describe how, as Earth orbits the Sun, different parts of Earth are tilted towards or away from the Sun. This is what creates changing seasons. For example, in the northern hemisphere, summer turns into autumn (fall), followed by winter. However, in the southern hemisphere, at the same time, winter turns to spring, then summer.

- Explain how, when the northern hemisphere is tilted away from the Sun, it is winter in the southern hemisphere. This is because the Sun's rays are more spread out, so daylight hours are shorter and the temperature is cooler.

- Give all learners **Worksheet 10.3** to complete.

Misconceptions

Some learners might think different seasons are caused by Earth being closer to or further away from the Sun. This can be explained as you talk about the degree of tilt of Earth's axis.

Digging deeper

Support: Use a globe to demonstrate Earth's rotation and a flashlight to model the Sun's rays shining on Earth to explain the seasons.

Extension: Ask these learners to carry out some research to find out why there are no seasons around the equator.

Wrapping up

- Talk through the answers to **Worksheet 10.3.**
1

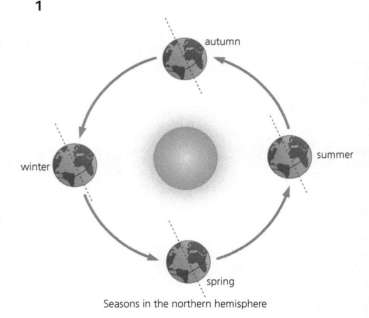

Seasons in the northern hemisphere

2

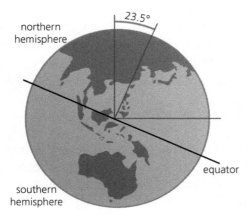

northern hemisphere

23.5°

equator

southern hemisphere

3 Look for answers that include ideas about when different parts of Earth are tilted towards or away from the Sun. This is what creates changing seasons.

10.4 Satellites

Resources

PowerPoint 10.4; Worksheet 10.4 (Boost); internet access or reference books about satellites and space junk

Starter activity

- Organise learners into pairs and ask them to discuss this question: *What is a satellite?*
- Discuss their responses and then use **PowerPoint 10.4**, slide 1, to show a clip about Earth and the Moon. Focus on the first part of the video about the Moon being a satellite of Earth, although the rest of the video contains some other interesting information about the phases of the Moon. The phases will be studied in detail in Stage 6.

Main activities

- Introduce the term 'natural satellite' and explain that this is an object which orbits a planet; hence the Moon is Earth's natural satellite.
- Explain how some of the planets have more than one moon (or satellite). For example, Jupiter is currently thought to have 79 moons or satellites. This has recently been overtaken by Saturn as the planet with the most moons. It is thought Saturn has 82 moons.
- Introduce the term 'artificial satellites' and explain that these are artificial objects orbiting Earth. They are made by humans and sent into space.
- Ask learners whether they can think of any artificial satellites. (They might be able to name weather stations, the International Space Station and/or communication satellites.) Use **PowerPoint 10.4**, slide 2, which shows an image of the International Space Station. Some learners might recognise this when they see the image.
- Ask learners what they think the term 'space junk' means or whether they know any examples of space junk. Explain that this is such things as

parts of old spacecraft, old and disused satellites or tools discarded while spacecraft have been repaired. Talk about how these things can be dangerous because they are whizzing about in space so quickly; they can cause harm to other spacecraft or to astronauts on spacewalks.

- Give all learners **Worksheet 10.4** to complete.

Misconceptions

Some learners might think the Moon is a planet. Using the example of the Moon as a natural satellite of Earth should help dispel this misconception.

Digging deeper

Support: Allow these learners to work in a small mixed-ability group to carry out the research. Alternatively, give them the name of a planet and its moons to research.

Extension: Ask these learners to research recent ideas for collecting space junk.

Assessment for learning/ Wrapping up

Ask the learners about their answers to the questions on **Worksheet 10.4**.

- **Answers:**
  1 an object which orbits a planet
  2 the Moon
  3 for example, Jupiter = 79 or Saturn = 82
  4 any from the International Space Station, weather satellites or communication satellites
  5 a natural satellite is any object orbiting a planet. An artificial satellite is made by humans and sent into space.
  6 junk floating around in space, such as old satellites or discarded parts from space shuttles/rockets

10 Unit assessment

Questions to ask

- *What one word can be used to describe the path of Earth's orbit around the Sun?*
- *What is the angle of tilt of Earth?*
- *Why do we have seasons?*

- *Name a natural satellite of Earth.*
- *What are artificial satellites?*
- *What is space junk?*

Summative assessment activities

Observe the learners while they complete these activities. You will be able to quickly identify those who appear to be confident and those who might need additional support.

The tilt of Earth

This activity provides an opportunity for learners to model their understanding to describe the position of Earth in space.

You will need:
Modelling clay; wooden skewer; protractor

What to do

- Ask learners to make a model of Earth with the modelling clay and to use the wooden skewer as Earth's axis.
- Ask them to point to the northern and southern hemispheres and the equator.
- Ask them which hemisphere they live in.
- Then ask them to use the protractor to set the angle of the Earth's tilt. Can they remember the actual angle of tilt? (They do not necessarily need to remember this.)
- Ask learners to explain how the tilt of Earth causes seasons to occur.

Seasons around the world

This activity provides learners with an opportunity to show their understanding of how seasons occur around the world.

You will need:
Modelling clay; globe; flashlight

What to do

- Ask the learner to place a piece of modelling clay on the globe on the country where they live or as requested by the teacher.
- Tell them to shine the flashlight from directly above the country.
- Describe the Sun's rays (as depicted by the flashlight) and the area they cover.
- Ask the learner to describe which season it would be in that place when the Sun is directly above.
- Ask learners to show what is different in winter and explain why.

Written assessment

Give learners time to complete **Worksheet 10.5**. They should work independently or with their usual in-class support.